THE EXPAT MONEY PLAYBOOK

THE EXPAT MONEY PLAYBOOK

Unlocking Your Passport to Wealth

ARIELLE TUCKER
CFP® and EA

WILEY

Published by John Wiley & Sons, Inc., Hoboken, New Jersey.

For general information on our other products and services or for technical support, please contact our Customer Care Department within the United States at (800) 762-2974, outside the United States at (317) 572-3993 or fax (317) 572-4002.

Wiley also publishes its books in a variety of electronic formats. Some content that appears in print may not be available in electronic formats. For more information about Wiley products, visit our web site at www.wiley.com.

Library of Congress Cataloging-in-Publication Data has been applied for:

Print ISBN: 9781394415953
ePUB ISBN: 9781394415960
ePDF ISBN: 9781394415977

Cover Design: Wiley
Cover Images: Anucha/stock.adobe.com, anna42f/stock.adobe.com

SKY10165187_081126

CONTENTS

NOTE TO THE READER

This is not a book about how to pick stocks, beat the market, or optimize your investment returns. There are plenty of excellent books that do that, and you should absolutely read them. But this isn't one of them.

This book is your financial playbook for moving abroad, grounded in real expat experience and designed to help you build, protect, and enjoy your life as a US expat.

It's written for people who are building a life outside the United States while still being legally, financially, and tax-connected to it. If you are a US citizen, a US green card holder, or otherwise treated as a US tax resident, your financial life follows a different set of rules than your non-US friends, neighbors, and colleagues abroad.

That difference matters more than most people realize.

Many Americans move abroad assuming they can simply "figure it out as they go" or that the financial advice they've always followed at home will still apply. Others take cues from expat friends or influencers who aren't subject to US tax rules at all. Both approaches can lead to unpleasant (and often costly) surprises.

The reason a cavalier approach to financial planning is risky when leaving the United States is that US citizens, US green card holders, and those treated as US tax residents are subject to a tax system known as citizenship-based taxation (CBT). This form of taxation dates from the Civil War period, when President Abraham Lincoln's administration applied it to ensure anyone physically leaving the country remained liable to financially contribute to the war effort.

Today, the United States is one of just two countries in the world to utilize this method of taxation; the vast majority apply residence-based taxation. Residence-based taxation (RBT) is conceptually much easier, and objectively, fairer in that, in general, if you're tax resident in an RBT country, you pay taxes there. If you're not a tax resident, then you don't.

The citizenship-based taxation rulebook is more complex, riddled with irritating "gotchas" even if you try to research and understand how to follow the rules. At a high level, if CBT applies to you, you remain tied to the US tax system, even when you live, work, invest, and retire elsewhere. With few exceptions, CBT requires you to continue filing a US tax return every year. Contrary to popular belief, this does not necessarily mean that you'll be double taxed on your income. In fact, many US expats don't owe any US tax at all, save for any costs associated with filing their "expat tax return" from abroad, such as working with an expat accountant.

All this to say, the rules around taxes, investments, retirement accounts, banking, reporting, healthcare, estate planning, and even basic financial access can change the moment you cross a border, and they don't always change in intuitive ways.

This book exists because the cross-border tax and financial reality for everyday US people is rarely explained in one place. And while it's impossible to cover a topic of this magnitude in-depth in just one book, the goal is to leave you feeling more equipped to ask the right questions and confident in your ability to make informed decisions based on the answers you get.

In a nutshell, this book will help you understand the following:

- Where Americans abroad commonly get tripped up
- How the rules around taxes and financial planning may change, or even stop working, once you move
- What decisions carry long-term consequences
- And when it's worth slowing down and engaging professional help

Most personal finance books assume a stationary life: one country, one tax system, one legal framework. This book assumes motion. It assumes your life may span multiple countries, currencies, and systems. I'm personally on a mission to normalize that reality because there are an estimated nine million Americans living abroad, and I'm one of them.

If you already live abroad, this book will help you review your current financial and tax framework and identify areas that deserve a second look. If you're planning a move, it will help you prepare intentionally instead of reactively. And if you're still in the dreaming phase, well, you're very obviously wading into the "research" phase if you're reading this book.

That all said, I want to say something that might sound paradoxical given my profession as a cross-border financial planner: you don't need to have everything figured out to live internationally. It all starts with understanding, at a baseline, that moving abroad comes with financial landmines to navigate. This book is here to equip you with the knowledge to not only recognize the landmines in your particular financial landscape but to educate you on how to go about calmly disarming them *before* they detonate.

PART I

THE DECISION TO LEAVE

CHAPTER ONE

WHY DO YOU WANT TO MOVE ABROAD?

Key Question: Why do you actually want to live abroad, and what are you willing to trade?

Most people don't start planning an international move with spreadsheets or visa checklists. They start with a daydream.

Maybe it's the kind of trip that follows you home, one where the air felt lighter, the days slower, and you caught yourself thinking, I could live like this. Maybe it's a phone you can't stop scrolling past, a friend who casually says, "We just moved to Spain," or a quiet, persistent feeling that the life you're living no longer quite fits. At the beginning, moving abroad feels aspirational, even romantic. Slower mornings. Better work-life balance. A different pace, something more.

And then the daydream does what it always does when it's serious: it turns into research.

Suddenly, you're Googling visas at midnight. You're deep in expat Facebook groups. You're scanning rental listings you can't read, comparing schools, reading healthcare threads, and trying to piece together what life might actually look like on the other side. That's when the logistics get loud: Visas. Taxes. Healthcare. Banking. Housing. Schools. The checklist is urgent, practical, and overwhelming, and it can make the entire idea feel either very real or very intimidating, very fast.

But here's what seasoned expats learn (usually the hard way): The strongest moves abroad don't start with logistics. They start with why.

Simon Sinek popularized this idea in his book *Start with Why*, where lasting decisions are built on purpose, not process. The same is true for moving abroad. Before you decide where you'll live or how you'll get a visa, you need to understand what you're actually moving for.

Not the Instagram version of your why. Not the fantasy. The honest one.

What are you running toward?

What are you willing to trade?

And what kind of life are you trying to build on the other side of the move?

Because moving abroad doesn't magically turn you into a new person. It turns the volume up on who you already are. If you're anxious, uncertainty can amplify it. If you avoid conflict, bureaucracy will find you. If you're burned out, a new country might give you breathing room, but it won't do the healing for you.

Moving abroad is not an escape hatch. It doesn't fix everything. It's a life decision.

And it's a hard one, just a different hard.

So, before you run, slow down. Before you plan, get honest. Start with why.

Expert Insights: Define What "Living Abroad" Looks Like to You

Most people start with the question: Where should I move?

But the more important question is: What do I want my life abroad to look like?

When someone says they want to move abroad, that vision can mean very different things. For some, it's slowing down and enjoying a more relaxed pace of life. For others, it's adventure, travel, or the chance to reinvent their career.

Moving abroad isn't just about living your current life in a different country. It's an opportunity to design a life that aligns more closely with how you actually want to live. Getting clear on that vision will guide many of your biggest decisions, from which country and city you choose to how you spend your time once you arrive.

To start shaping that vision, ask yourself:

What pace of life do you want?

How important are community, culture, or language in your experience abroad?

Do you want a walkable city, a slower pace of life, or proximity to nature?

Are you optimizing for lifestyle, cost of living, career opportunities, or overall quality of life?

One mistake many future expats make is trying to replicate someone else's dream life abroad. The most successful moves happen when you design a life that fits your priorities, values, and stage of life.

Once you have a clear vision of what you want, you can reverse-engineer a path to get there.

—Cepee Tabibian, Founder, She Hit Refresh

WHY "WHY" MATTERS MORE THAN EVER

In recent years, more Americans have been openly exploring life outside the United States for political reasons, economic pressure, healthcare costs, safety concerns, lifestyle, adventure, or a desire to raise children differently. One 2025 Harris Poll found that 44% of Americans have seriously considered retiring abroad.

And interest isn't limited to retirees. Gallup reporting has highlighted that women are more likely than men to say they'd like to leave the United States permanently, reflecting a broader pattern of "wish vs. plan" in relocation thinking.

But interest and readiness are not the same thing. A meaningful share of people *consider* the idea without taking steps because once you get past the highlight reel, international life asks for a level of effort, patience, and adaptability that you can't outsource.

This is why we start here.

If your "why" is clear, you can tolerate the chaos that comes with becoming a beginner again, new systems, new norms, new rules, new language, new trade-offs.

If your "why" is vague, every obstacle starts to feel like evidence that you made the wrong decision.

RUN TOWARD SOMETHING, NOT ONLY AWAY

It's human to want to leave when you feel exhausted, disillusioned, or unsafe. But if your only reason to move is "to escape," you may arrive abroad and discover you brought the same stress with you, plus immigration paperwork.

Politics is a good example. If the only thing holding up your decision is a political moment, remember this: political seasons change. And many countries that look calm from a distance have their own versions of division, bureaucracy, and restrictions, sometimes more intense, not less.

A durable "why" has at least two parts:

- **What you want more of:** time, safety, community, walkability, healthcare access, family support, slower pace, career freedom, adventure, autonomy
- **What you're willing to give up:** income growth, convenience, language comfort, proximity to family, cultural familiarity, certain foods, certain services, the ease of "knowing how things work"

That second part is the part most people skip. It's also the part that determines whether you stay.

THE VALUES-FIRST EXPAT EXERCISE

To help you get oriented and more deeply understand your personal reasons for wanting to move abroad, this can be a useful exercise to do, either by yourself or with whomever you plan to move. Note that what surfaces during initial reflections can vary drastically from what surfaces during reflections even a few months later, so the emphasis should be on getting your thoughts down on paper. There is no "right" answer; the goal should just be to answer honestly.

For example, many Americans have been trained to associate their self-worth with the type of job they do or the number of hours they work. Is this a metric you want to continue abiding by when you move abroad? If not, get real with yourself. Challenge yourself to put pen to paper, even if what you write is, "I want to work no more than 20 hours a week and will consider myself financially secure if I can comfortably afford my dream lifestyle in the French countryside."

Step 1: Your "Pull" and Your "Push"

Write two short lists:

- **Pull—What I'm running toward:**
  What would be meaningfully better in my day-to-day life abroad?
- **Push—What I'm trying to reduce:**
  What feels unsustainable about life right now?

Now underline anything that is internal (burnout, loneliness, anxiety, lack of boundaries, feeling directionless). Those things don't automatically disappear with a new zip code. They deserve their own plan.

Step 2: Your Top Five Values (Pick, Don't Rank)

Choose **five** values that you want your life to reflect for the next three to five years. Examples would be stability, freedom, family, health, community, growth, simplicity, adventure, security, belonging, autonomy, service, creativity, learning, etc.

Now, for each value, finish this sentence:

- **"I'll know this value is present when …"**

Example:

- *Value: Health*
- "I'll know this value is present when I'm getting 7+ hours of sleep a night, found a spin class I love and attend twice a week, and don't feel chronically on edge."

This turns values into something you can actually measure.

Step 3: The Trade-off Test

For each of your five values, answer:

- **What am I willing to trade to protect this value abroad?**
- **What am I not willing to trade?**

Example:

- "I'm willing to trade apartment size for walkability."
- "I'm not willing to trade proximity to medical care."

This is where your destination list gets real.

Step 4: Your "Chaos Budget"

Moving abroad costs money, but it also comes with real, often overlooked costs to your emotional energy and mental bandwidth, especially during periods of uncertainty and transition.

Rate each category 1–10 (10 = very strong right now):

- Energy and capacity
- Relationship resilience (partner/family alignment)
- Acceptance of uncertainty
- Administration tolerance (forms, appointments, waiting)
- Social confidence (building community from scratch)

If any category is below a 5, your plan needs more runway: more savings, more time, more support, or a slower timeline.

Step 5: Write Your Why Statement (Two Sentences)

Use this template:

"I am moving abroad to __________, because __________.

I will know it's working when __________."

Example:

"I am moving abroad to build a more walkable, community-centered life because my current routine feels expensive and isolating. I will know it's working when I spend more time outside, rely less on my car, and feel connected to people weekly."

PS: Even in this example, you don't necessarily need to move to another country to accomplish this. So, dig deep.

OPTIONAL: AI PROMPTS YOU CAN USE

Moving abroad is a very personal process. While some people may prefer to leave their phone in another room, light a candle, and curl up on the couch with a pen and paper, others may find that working with an interactive tool can facilitate organizing their thoughts. With that, the following AI prompts are designed so you can copy/paste into ChatGPT or another large language model.

Prompt 1: Clarify my "why"

"Interview me to clarify my reasons for moving abroad. Ask 10 questions one at a time. After my answers, summarize my top three motivations, my top three hidden risks, and the trade-offs I seem most willing and unwilling to make."

Prompt 2: Values to lifestyle translation

"Here are my top five values and what they mean to me: [paste your values exercise]. Translate these into a realistic 'expat lifestyle definition' with daily/weekly indicators and list the most likely ways I could sabotage them unintentionally. If you need more information on me as a person in order to help me understand where I might fall prey to self-sabotage, follow up with thoughtful questions like a psychologist specialized in cognitive-behavioral therapy in order to provide the most helpful response."

Prompt 3: Partner alignment (if relevant)

"Act as a neutral facilitator. Ask me and my partner (we'll answer separately) questions to uncover misalignment about money, social life, pace of life, career, family proximity, and risk tolerance. Then produce a one-page summary of alignment, friction points, and compromises to test."

Prompt 4: The destination reality check

"My shortlist is [countries/cities]. Based on my values, preferences, constraints, and risk tolerance, [paste], tell me what I'm likely underestimating, what I may be over-romanticizing, and what questions I must answer before choosing a destination."

TURNING YOUR "WHY" INTO A PLAN: SMART GOALS FOR MOVING ABROAD

Once you're clear on *why* you want to move abroad, the next step is turning that clarity into action. This is where many expat dreams quietly stall. A strong "why" creates motivation, but without structure, it can remain abstract for years. This is where SMART goals come in.

SMART goals, an approach to goal setting created by George T. Doran in 1981 with initial application to writing effective management goals, aren't about rigidity or perfection.

In the context of planning a move abroad, they're about translating a life vision into steps that can survive real life, bureaucracy, and uncertainty. They help you separate what's aspirational from what's actionable. SMART stands for Specific, Measurable, Achievable, Realistic, and Time-Bound.

Let's break each one down through the lens of moving abroad.

S—Specific: What Exactly Are You Trying to Do?

A vague goal like "*move abroad someday*" may feel emotionally resonant, but it doesn't give you a lot of material with which to actually build yourself a runway to move abroad. Setting specific goals related to your interest in moving will help you to define the shape of the life you're imagining.

Ask yourself:

- Where are you moving?
- What are the immigration avenues available to you to move to that particular country?
- What is the primary purpose of your move: work, family, lifestyle, education, temporary sabbatical (intend to return), temporary sabbatical (open to staying long-term), or retirement?

Unspecific: "I want to live in Europe."

Specific: "I want to move to Spain on a nonlucrative visa and live there for at least two years. I don't feel like I can commit to moving permanently at this point, so I am approaching this as a temporary sabbatical from my life in the United States."

Getting specific can feel challenging or constraining, but it's important to remember that, paradoxically, asking yourself these questions is how you set yourself up to weather the way the answers will change over time.

Because they will change, and you can either be mentally prepared for the changes that will occur in your psychology and value system, or you can be unprepared and wind up feeling even more adrift than you did initially, and that's a feeling you want to avoid.

M—Measurable: How Will You Know You're Making Progress?

Moving abroad doesn't happen in one big leap. Rather, doing so requires intentionally executing a series of small, sometimes unglamorous steps. Measurable goals help you recognize progress even when the finish line feels far away.

Following are examples of measurable expat goals:

- Speaking to your employer about an expat contract or the ability to work remotely
- Saving a defined relocation fund (e.g., $30,000)
- Completing language coursework to a specific level
- Submitting a visa application
- Spending 90 days in your target country on a trial stay
- Reducing US-based financial ties (closing accounts, selling property, etc.)

Not measurable:

"I'm preparing financially."

Measurable:

"I have opened a multi-currency (ex, Interactive Brokers, Wise, Revolut) account and will build a six-month emergency fund in euros before applying for my visa."

Measurable goals create momentum, and momentum matters when the process gets frustrating.

A—Achievable: Is This Possible with Your Current Constraints?

Achievable doesn't mean "easy." It means honest. An achievable goal considers the following:

- Citizenship or residency options
- Income requirements
- Life stage
- Family/spousal responsibilities
- Health considerations
- Career realities

For example, moving abroad as a single freelancer is very different from moving with school-aged children or aging parents. However, one of the cornerstone features of successful expats is their adaptability, which is to say that if you're finding your first attempt at a move-abroad plan is starting to feel a bit, "square peg, round hole," it may be a matter of reevaluating one of the core components, such as the target country.

Not achievable (for now):

"I'll move to Portugal on the D7 visa and figure out how to manage my US retirement distributions once I'm there."

Achievable:

"I'll confirm that the D7 visa pathway is the best option for me and connect with US expat tax and possibly a cross-border advisor specialized in working with Americans in Portugal to evaluate my particular situation and help me create a plan to move that is tax optimal and ensures the lowest-possible lifetime tax bill."

Achievable goals build confidence. Unrealistic ones create burnout before you ever leave.

R—Realistic: Does This Fit the Life You Actually Want?

This is the most overlooked part of goal setting and the most important for expats.

A goal can be achievable and still wrong for *you*.

Being realistic means accounting for the following:

- Your tolerance for uncertainty—and recognizing that you can increase this tolerance over time, but it will take conscious and sustained effort on your part
- Bureaucracy and language barriers
- Distance from family
- Healthcare systems
- Cultural differences
- Income volatility
- Loneliness and community building

Not realistic:

"I'll move to a small town in Tuscany and live like a local immediately, even though I don't speak the language and am easily frustrated by inefficiency."

Realistic:

"I'll move to Florence, where there is a lively expat community, which will offset the initial loneliness and sense of displacement that's common for expats in the first year or two. I will budget for private healthcare, language classes, and support services during my first year to reduce stress and take trips into the surrounding countryside to explore potential villages to move to once I've adjusted to the initial change of living in Italy."

In essence, a realistic goal supports the life you're trying to build, not the version of yourself you wish you could just will yourself to be at the drop of a hat.

T—Time-bound: When Is This Happening?

Without a timeline, goals drift. With a timeline, decisions become clearer.

Time-bound goals don't need a single fixed date, but they do need a window.

Consider these examples:

- Within the next 12 months
- Before my child starts middle school
- By the end of 2030
- After one more promotion cycle

Not time-bound:

> "Eventually, we'll move abroad."

Time-bound:

> "We plan to relocate within 24–36 months, depending on visa approval."

Timelines force prioritization. They also make it easier to say no to things that don't align with your bigger plan.

PUTTING IT ALL TOGETHER: A SMART EXPAT GOAL EXAMPLE

Goal: "In the next 24 months, we will relocate to Portugal on a D7 visa by building a €40,000 relocation reserve, maintaining qualifying passive income, completing a 90-day trial stay, and securing international healthcare coverage, while keeping one US account active for reentry flexibility. We will explore relocation services and decide whether we feel more comfortable moving with professional support or whether we are comfortable in our ability to DIY the process. We will maintain the contact information of expert hand holders in case we get overwhelmed and require professional support in the end."

That's not just a dream. That's a plan.

WHY SMART GOALS MATTER FOR EXPATS

I mentioned earlier that one of the key markers of a successful expat is their ability to adapt. Setting SMART goals is one way to recognize your current capacity to handle change and challenge while providing a framework to revisit as you evolve once you've moved. Make no mistake: there will be trying moments when you move abroad. A major example that comes to mind here is the end of Portugal's Non-Habitual Residence regime, which allowed qualifying foreigners to move to Portugal and benefit from an incredible tax benefit. However, this regime is now over, and many people who are moving to Portugal (or even currently in Portugal) are unaware of the massive differences in preparation that are now needed on the financial side to move smartly. (See what I did there?)

Again, SMART goals don't eliminate uncertainty, but they give you a framework sturdy enough to adapt when things don't go exactly as planned. Once your why is clear and your goals are grounded, everything else in this book, tax planning, healthcare, housing, budgeting, and long-term strategy, has something solid to attach to.

Next, we'll build from these goals into concrete financial and logistical planning so that your move isn't just intentional, but sustainable.

If you skipped this chapter hoping to "get to the practical stuff," that urge will come back later, usually when something feels harder than expected.

Return here when the following happens:

- You feel stuck.
- You're second-guessing a destination.
- You and a partner feel misaligned.
- The process feels heavier than it should.

YOUR "WHY" READINESS CHECKLIST

Before you move on to visas, taxes, and logistics, pause here.

You don't need certainty. You need clarity.

Use this checklist as a gut check, not a test you have to "pass." If you can answer most of these honestly, you're ready to move forward. If several feel unclear, that's a sign that you may want to revisit those parts of the exercise or perhaps have an open dialogue with a trusted family member or friend.

> **Pro Tip**: Sometimes having a discussion with someone who is fully certain they would never move abroad can be useful in helping you get clear on certain questions that feel difficult to answer without external opinions. For example, maybe your friend who could never see herself leaving the United States mentions that she could never "uproot her children," and you realize with sudden sureness that you don't see moving abroad as destabilizing; you see it as an opportunity to expand your and your family's horizons. Now that would fit into the SMART framework well.

Your Why

- I can clearly articulate *what I'm running toward*, not just what I'm leaving.
- I understand which of my motivations are internal vs. external.
- I've considered whether my goals require a move abroad or something else entirely.

Your Values

- I've identified my top five values for the next three to five years.
- I can describe what those values look like in daily life, not just in theory.
- I know which values are nonnegotiable and which are flexible.

Your Trade-offs

- I've named what I'm willing to give up to protect my values.
- I've named what I'm *not* willing to sacrifice, even for the move.
- I understand that every destination is a bundle of trade-offs, not a solution.

Your Capacity

- I've assessed my current energy, flexibility, and administrative tolerance honestly.
- I've built (or plan to build) enough runway, time, savings, support for my capacity level.
- I accept that needing help or more time is part of a sustainable plan.

Your Direction

- I can write a 1–2 sentence "why statement" without overexplaining.
- I've translated that why into at least one SMART goal.
- I have a rough timeline, even if it's flexible.

If this checklist feels grounding rather than overwhelming, you're ready to take the next step.

> **Expat Reflection:** *Living abroad is a new life stage, full of milestones, thrill, and yes, loss. Each place is a new chapter. Don't reinvent the wheel unless you have to: learn from those who've done it before, not just for information, but for wisdom. Few experiences give you this kind of chance to re imagine yourself and step deeper into the mystery. Enjoy the ride, it will change you in ways you can't imagine, if you let it.*
>
> *—Mickelle Weber, Founder House of Peregrine*

CHAPTER TWO

HOW DO YOU PREPARE TO MOVE ABROAD WHEN YOU DON'T KNOW WHAT YOU DON'T KNOW?

Key Question: What should I do before moving abroad?

It's incredibly easy to romanticize a move abroad—especially if you've never done it. That's not me being patronizing; it's me typing while remembering how eager I was to just "learn what I had to do" before packing my bags when I got my husband on board with us moving and set about learning what had to be done, with the mentality that moving to a new country can be distilled to a single checklist. (*Oh, how wrong I was.*)

One of the most important things to realize before and during your research it that *you don't know what you don't know.*

And everything you don't know will need to be identified and sorted into a separate list.

Let's look at one of the first things people think about when it comes to moving, whether it's down the block or across an ocean: things.

Clothes, personal effects, identification documents, perhaps furniture—these are all obvious things to inventory and decide what to do with.

There are also some obvious logistical starting points, such as making sure that your passport is up to date, the immigration pathway you're eyeing has been confirmed as both doable and that best path for you, and you have either a scouting trip or places already in mind to move to.

Expert Insight: *There are six stages to moving abroad: Ideation, Planning, Exploration, Paperwork, Logistics, and Settling In.*

The first mistake we see people make is doing the stages out of order, like choosing a country to move to before they've established whether they meet the requirements. It's a frustrating waste of time and money to backtrack in the process.

The second mistake is trying to tackle all six stages at once: learning a language, packing boxes, searching for homes, gathering paperwork, and more. It's overwhelming, and it can also be a distraction from less pleasant tasks you've got to get through.

—Jen Barnett, CEO of Expatsi

CAUTION: US FINANCES CAN QUICKLY FEEL LIKE A HOUSE OF HORRORS WHEN TRYING TO UNDERSTAND WHAT THEY MEAN IN A CROSS-BORDER CONTEXT

Less obvious to most is to consider how the local taxation, savings and investment schemes, social insurances, and retirement systems in your new place of residence interact with the US system, to which you will very likely retain various financial and reporting obligations. As such, your lack of awareness (as well as that of your nonspecialized financial advisor, more on this later) can have very expensive and long-term consequences that affect your savings and retirement income.

The good news is that you don't need to figure it all out alone. This chapter is your comprehensive pre-move checklist, part financial strategy, part legal survival guide, and part "learn from everyone else's mistakes so you don't make the same ones."

Think of it like this: if moving abroad were a marathon, this chapter is your training plan. You need to break the process down into manageable steps and intentionally build in rest days. Set unreasonable expectations and hustle through downtime, and you'll be the person hobbling along at mile 18, wondering if you'll even be able to finish the race. Follow it, and you'll arrive in your new country ready to hit the ground running (or at least confidently navigating the local grocery store without crying in aisle three).

STEP 1: TAKE STOCK OF YOUR FINANCIAL HOME

While this is an exercise we should all be doing with some regularity, the truth is that life happens. We fall behind on tracking where money is going and how it's being spent—and trying to understand just how many streaming services and apps you're subscribed to can feel like an impossible task (although there are tools to streamline the latter, FYI).

So before looking at the following list through the hyper-specific and quite critical "move abroad" lens, I invite you to take a breath and consider it against the current state of your financial house. Getting the information in order and your mind wrapped around where things stand on the US side is the first part of the financial planning puzzle, because you can't financially plan for a move abroad if you don't know what numbers you're working with.

- **Review your current finances:** Create a Google or Excel Sheet and list all your accounts (bank, retirement, credit cards, loans). You'd be surprised how many people forget about a random 401(k) from a previous employer or a dusty savings account opened when they were young. Make a plan for how to consolidate the "easy" stuff initially, such as scheduling time to contact your bank about consolidating your 401(k) accounts or closing old savings accounts. Be careful about overconsolidation at this stage, though; depending on where you're moving and through which immigration pathway, it will be important to put your US accounts through a cross-border evaluation to ensure you're not triggering avoidable (and, often, expensive) foreign tax issues (for example: moving to Portugal as a retiree with all of your money in pre-tax retirement accounts).
- **Open an international-friendly bank account:** Look for global banks or fintechs (like Wise, Revolut, or HSBC) that were designed to handle cross-border transfers efficiently. You don't want to be stuck

paying a $40 fee each time you need to move your own money around or waiting for days for a transfer to be completed. During this stage, I also recommend familiarizing yourself with the names of foreign banks in your target country. Which Spanish banks are the local, institutional equivalents of Chase, Charles Schwab, or Capital One?

- **Credit cards: streamline and strategize:** Cancel cards you don't need but keep at least one with no foreign transaction fees. Popular cards include the Chase Sapphire Reserve and Capital One Venture X, among others. For the most up-to-date recommendations, NerdWallet is a trusty resource, but bear in mind that their recommendations assume you live in the United States, so many of the benefits won't apply if you move abroad. If you're moving in the next 6–12 months, consider applying for a travel rewards card *before* you move, since approvals are much easier while you still have a US address and credit history, and many cards offer a generous sign-up bonus paid in points if you spend a certain amount within a predefined period. If you are taking advantage of a corporate relocation package, consider that many (potentially large) expenses will flow through your credit card on their path to reimbursement. Think of this as your "golden window" for collecting bonus points.

Pro Tips

- Online forums such as Facebook groups and Reddit can be helpful here in sourcing not just the name of local banks, but specific branches in your target city because, for reasons you'll soon learn, many Americans experience difficulty opening a local bank account, and it's not uncommon for local banks to simply refuse to take on a US client.
- Don't assume you can easily open a new US credit card from abroad; it's often impossible without a US address or phone number.

STEP 2: TAX PLANNING AND EXIT STRATEGIES

Tax planning before moving abroad is perhaps one of the most misunderstood topics in the expat space because so much depends on your specific situation. A single retiree from Wisconsin planning to permanently relocate to France via a long-stay visitor visa will have an *entirely different* set of considerations from a young, self-employed couple relocating from California to Portugal with their toddler and another child on the way. Truly, the importance of connecting with a reputable expat tax professional who specializes in working with Americans in your target country cannot be understated if you value your financial health.

Here are just a few things to consider at the outset of your tax planning:

- **Understand US tax obligations:** As I mentioned in the introduction, Americans don't escape the IRS just because they moved abroad. The US's citizenship-based taxation regime means that you'll likely need to keep filing US tax returns regardless of where you live or make your money, even if you owe nothing. Indeed, it's often beneficial to continue filing after you move, no matter what, especially if you have children.
- **State tax ties:** Some states (looking at you, California, Massachusetts, and New York) make it, ahem, complicated to cut ties. In addition to an expat tax specialist versed in working with Americans in your target country, ideally, this individual will also be able to support a strategic tax exit from the local and state tax level too, where possible.
- **Ask about exit taxes:** If you're giving up a US green card or US citizenship, you may owe an "exit tax." It's like the cover charge no one told you about at the world's most expensive club. It's not as simple as shredding your passport. Get professional advice before making this decision.

STEP 3: HEALTHCARE, INSURANCE, AND HOUSING

There's a reason that healthcare, insurance, and administrative meetings with a local real estate agency don't typically make the Instagram highlight reel of life abroad. But I would argue that these elements of "expat life" deserve just as much attention as your feed-worthy adventures.

Healthcare

Does your new country offer public health insurance? Will you need private coverage (as is common for many visa types in the first year, at least)? Can you keep your current plan temporarily, and does it provide coverage abroad? These are questions to ask and know the answer to *before* you leave and need to see a doctor, and it's typically clarified as what's required during the visa application process.

Insurance

Beyond health, think renters, homeowners, life, legal, umbrella/liability, and disability. Policies don't always transfer across borders, and in many localities, coverage is compulsory.

Housing

Will you rent, buy, or stay short term until you get the lay of the land? Understand the local rental market and deposit rules. In some countries, it is customary to ask for six months' rent upfront, and in others, you may experience difficulty renting as a foreigner unless you're able to prove and provide funds beyond what's typically required. The latter is, of course, unfair, but it's a good example of how many things are simply more difficult when you're abroad, and you just have to roll with it and adapt.

STEP 4: LEGAL PAPERWORK (THE BORING BUT CRITICAL STUFF)

In the cross-border financial planning community, whenever we meet with someone planning to move abroad, one of the first questions we ask is, "What immigration pathway are you taking?" Put another way, visas, permits, and contracts are the backbone of your move, defining the reality within which tax and financial planning can take shape.

For this reason, it's extremely important to be confident that you're moving on the most optimal immigration route for your situation. For example, the long-stay visitor visa in France has historically had a reputation for being an under-the-table digital nomad visa of sorts, but in recent years, French tax authorities and legislators have begun scrutinizing this immigration route, all but ensuring that anyone actively earning income on the long-stay visitor will be subject to scrutiny in some capacity—and if the tax authorities come for you first, the immigration department that approved your visa won't be of any help.

So, what should you consider when evaluating and building the legal framework of your move?

Visas and Residency Permits

Every country has different requirements. Some want proof of sufficient savings and income, while others demand you already have a job lined up.

Take time to understand the restrictions of the visa you will be on: Can you change job titles or employers? Will your spouse be allowed to work? Research this *early* because bureaucracy doesn't move fast.

Contracts

Employment, rental, even cell phone, and gym contracts each come with specific notice periods and conditions for termination, leaving you financially responsible. Don't sign anything you don't understand; get translations if needed.

> **Expert Insight:** *Change your mindset before you change your country.*
>
> *One of the biggest challenges Americans face when moving abroad isn't always legal or tax-related, it's adjusting to how administrative systems work.*
>
> *In the United States, many processes are built around speed, flexibility, and problem-solving. If something goes wrong, there is often a way to fix it later. In many other countries, however, systems are far more* ***formal, document-driven, and procedure-oriented****.*
>
> *Being "substantively right" may not be enough. What matters is having the* **correct document, in the correct format, submitted through the correct process and at the correct time***. Missing paperwork, incorrect forms, or incomplete applications can delay approvals for weeks, or even months.*
>
> *For this reason, avoid making major life decisions that depend on administrative processes moving quickly. Do not assume issues can easily be corrected later, and recognize that navigating bureaucracy abroad*

(Continued)

(Continued)

> *often requires more preparation and patience than many Americans are used to.*
>
> *Once you understand how the system works, however, the process usually becomes much easier. Many countries, including Spain, offer tremendous long-term benefits for expats, such as strong public healthcare systems, improved work-life balance, safer communities, and access to broader regional economic opportunities. For many Americans, these advantages ultimately outweigh the initial bureaucratic hurdles.*
>
> *—Carlos Lorenzo, LLM, Founder, American & Legal Spain*

STEP 5: YOUR US FINANCIAL FOOTPRINT ABROAD

Here's something encouraging: US credit cards can continue to work for you, even after you move abroad, if you're strategic.

- **Travel rewards cards:** Apply before your move. A good rewards card can mean free flights home, hotel stays, or upgrades when you need them most. US credit cards are famously generous with perks compared to many countries, where limits are often low and rewards are nearly nonexistent. Considering that most expats will return to the US periodically to visit family and friends, those long-haul flights may help you quickly rack up points.
- **Keep a US address (for now, if possible):** US cards are tied to your US credit history and mailing address. If you close every account the

day you move, you'll make life harder if you ever decide to return. I generally recommend keeping a US address (family, trusted friend, or mail service) for at least the first two years abroad. This keeps the door open if you need to rebuild your US financial life. If your cards or accounts use two-factor authentication to log in online, make sure that it's linked to an account (email, phone number, authenticator app) that you will still have access to after you move. If you neglect this final step, you could be depending on waiting for whoever's phone number the credit card is connected to wake up and provide you the PIN for every transaction you need to make (ugh).

- **Expect limitations abroad:** Even with the best intentions, some US banks and card companies will eventually "kick you out" once they realize you're permanently abroad. It's not personal; it's compliance. Many financial institutions simply aren't set up to manage the regulatory burden of US expats. That's why you should start building your financial life abroad sooner rather than later: open a local bank account, get a local credit card, and gradually diversify your financial footprint so it's global, not US-centric.
- **Pro move: Freeze your credit (if moving permanently):** Consider freezing your credit with Experian, Equifax, and TransUnion. Identity theft is a global sport, and from overseas, you might not spot fraud quickly. Freezing your credit makes it nearly impossible for scammers to open new accounts in your name. Think of it as locking your US financial house before you go build your new one abroad.

QUICK CHECKLIST

- Review and consolidate bank accounts.
- Open international-friendly accounts.

- Streamline credit cards, strategically open a new travel card, if possible.
- Check US tax obligations and state residency.
- Explore healthcare and insurance options.
- Research visa and residency requirements.
- Understand rental contracts and housing deposits.
- Apply for any points/bonus cards before leaving.
- Make arrangements to keep a US mailing address, in consultation with your US expat tax advisor.
- Freeze your US credit (if it makes sense for you).

Final Word

Moving abroad is a uniquely exhilarating and overwhelming experience. You don't have to predict everything, but you *do* need a plan. Think of this checklist as your seatbelt: it won't prevent the bumps, but it will keep you safe as you accelerate into your new adventure.

Expert Insight: *There is one conversation I seem to have over and over with both prospects and existing clients. Discussing their goal of finding a "perfect city" to relocate.*

A lot of Americans when they start thinking about moving to Europe, always have a picture in mind of what life will look like. That image is often shaped by movies, social media, and influencers showing beautiful "filtered" versions of that life abroad. The cafes always look perfect, the streets are charming, and every sunset looks like a postcard.

The reality is that relocation is never that perfect. I often have calls with clients talking about moving to a new city after their first year abroad.

You might spend ten days in the south of Portugal during the summer and absolutely love it. The weather is great, the restaurants are full, and the town feels lively. But living there during the winter can feel very different. Things slow down, the town gets quiet, and what once felt charming might start to feel a bit boring.

That's why my advice is always about leaving yourself room for mistakes. If you move expecting everything to be perfect, then when you start noticing small problems, they can quickly feel overwhelming. It can even make you feel a bit trapped, like you made the wrong decision.

Instead, treat the first year as a period of exploration. Travel around. Visit different regions. Give yourself time before fully settling into a routine. What feels exciting during a short visit may not be the place where you ultimately feel most at home.

What I believe helps a successful move is about having a sense of purpose. Building connections with people around you. Getting involved in the community. Spending time understanding the local culture.

Moving abroad is about building a life that feels like home. And finding your home inside another home takes time, so don't rush it.

—Ricardo Jesus, MBA, Liberty Atlantic Advisors

CHAPTER THREE

HOW MUCH DOES IT REALLY COST TO MOVE AND LIVE ABROAD?

Key Question: What are the hidden costs of moving and living overseas?

For many Americans, moving abroad starts with a seductive idea: *Life will be cheaper.*

And most of the time, that's true. Rent is lower. Healthcare is affordable. Dinner out doesn't require a second mortgage. But just as often, the reality is more complicated.

Living abroad can absolutely lower your cost of living, but it can also **rearrange** your expenses in ways that catch people off guard. Some costs disappear entirely. Others multiply. And a few show up only after you've committed to the move and unpacked your suitcases.

This chapter isn't about scaring you off. It's about replacing vague assumptions with clear-eyed planning.

Because the question isn't whether living abroad is "cheaper" or "more expensive." The real question is: Cheaper or more expensive than what and for whom?

Your age, family situation, destination country, visa type, lifestyle choices, and even your tolerance for inconvenience all play a role. A single freelancer in Mexico will have a very different financial experience than a family of four in Zurich or a retiree in France.

In this chapter, we'll walk through the real costs of moving and living abroad, both the obvious ones and the sneaky ones—so you can build a budget that reflects real life, not just Instagram reels.

SECTION 1: THE TRUE COST OF MOVING

Most people dramatically underestimate the upfront cost of relocating abroad.

Flights are the easy part. It's everything that comes before boarding and after takeoff that adds up.

Relocation and Setup Costs

Even a relatively "light" move can include the following:

- Visa and residency application fees
- Legal translations, notarizations, apostilles
- Immigration lawyers and/or relocation consultants
- Temporary housing while you search for something permanent
- Storage costs in the United States
- Shipping household contents, or replacing items you don't bring

Some of these are one-time expenses. Others linger longer than expected.

For example, temporary housing often costs far more per month than long-term rent. Many expats plan for one or two months of short-term accommodation, and in tight housing markets may end up staying four or five months.

The Housing Deposit Shock

In many countries, landlords require the following:

- Three months' rent as a security deposit; we recommend ensuring this is in a blocked account that requires both you and your landlord to sign off on the release of the funds.
- Agency fees or administrative charges are especially common if using a relocation agency or real estate agent for your search.

That may mean you could be asked to pay three to five months of rent upfront, before you've even bought groceries.

> **Planning tip:** Your moving budget should include readily accessible cash in local currency, not just a total estimated cost. Large, one-time payments are common in the first weeks abroad.

Reality Check: Housing Scams Are Common and Expensive

When you're relocating abroad, housing scams become much easier to fall for and much harder to undo. Scammers know expats are under time pressure, unfamiliar with local norms, and eager to secure housing quickly.

A single bad decision here can cost you thousands of dollars.

The safest rule of thumb is simple: Never send money for housing you haven't verified in person or through a trusted, professional proxy.

Common Red Flags to Watch For

Be especially cautious if you notice any of the following:

- Unrealistically low pricing compared to similar listings in the area
- Pressure tactics, such as urgency to "act now" or threats that the property will disappear if you don't pay immediately
- No in-person viewing, with excuses like the landlord being "out of town" or unable to arrange a tour
- Suspicious payment requests, including gift cards, cryptocurrency, wire transfers, cash requests, or demands of any funds before signing a lease.
- Poor or vague communication (that isn't due to a language barrier), generic photos, unprofessional emails, or inconsistent details across listings
- Unexpected upfront fees, especially before a formal lease or contract exists

If something feels rushed, secretive, or unusually generous, pause. Scams often rely on urgency and confusion. You don't need to be a local to know when something doesn't feel right.

Protect Yourself

Our goal here is not to make you paranoid, but to ensure you are aware. Before signing on the dotted line or transferring cash, take care to do the following:

- Verify the agent or owner: Confirm licenses through official registries where applicable and check property ownership through public records when available.
- Research the listing: Use reverse image searches on photos, compare details across platforms, and watch for copied descriptions.

- Inspect in person (or via live video call): Never send money without seeing the property yourself or having a trusted local contact or licensed professional view it live.
- Use secure, traceable payment methods only: Legitimate landlords and agencies use bank transfers, secure portals, or escrow, not gift cards, crypto, or informal cash requests.
- Get everything in writing: Deposits, fees, lease terms, and move-in dates should be clearly spelled out in a formal, legally valid contract before any money changes hands.
- Protect your personal data: Be cautious about sharing sensitive information early in the process. Legitimate providers won't ask for excessive documentation before a contract exists.

Housing abroad often requires large upfront payments, and scammers know it. Slow down, verify details, and work with trusted professionals to ensure your relocation budget is protected.

Start Temporary to Protect Yourself

Housing scams are one of the strongest arguments for starting with temporary furnished housing when you move abroad. Reputable short-term rental platforms often provide built-in protections, verified listings, and some form of insurance or dispute resolution, features that are rarely available in private, long-term rentals.

While temporary housing usually comes at a premium, it allows you to take time to get oriented, evaluate neighborhoods on the ground, and make an informed, unrushed decision about a long-term lease. This matters because long-term rentals abroad often require large upfront payments, such as security deposits, agency fees, or several months of rent in advance.

Temporary rentals typically require little to no additional security deposit beyond the booking itself, reducing both financial exposure and scam risk. Think of the higher short-term cost as a form of insurance: you're buying time, flexibility, and protection while you learn how the local housing market actually works. More on this later.

SECTION 2: COMPARING THE COSTS OF LIVING ABROAD

You've probably seen cost-of-living comparisons claiming your destination is "20% cheaper than the United States" or that you can "live like a king for half the price."

Those numbers aren't necessarily wrong, but they're often incomplete.

Cost-of-living indexes are built on averages. And as an expat, your life rarely looks like the average local's.

The Basket Problem

Most cost-of-living comparisons are based on a standardized "basket" of goods and services: housing, groceries, transportation, healthcare, utilities, and a handful of lifestyle expenses. The problem is that *your* basket as an expat is often very different.

Many expats spend less than they did in the United States on things like healthcare, public transportation, and everyday dining, especially in countries with strong public systems or affordable local restaurants. Childcare and education can also be significantly cheaper in some places, depending on whether you use public or private options.

At the same time, expats often spend more in other areas. Housing in expat-friendly neighborhoods tends to come at a premium. Imported foods, specialty items, or familiar brands can cost far more than local alternatives. Private healthcare, international schools, and regular trips back to the United States can quietly add thousands to your annual budget.

So yes, you might save a few hundred dollars a month on groceries or transportation, while spending several thousand dollars a year on flights home. Both things can be true at the same time.

Lifestyle Inflation, Expat Style

There's also a subtler dynamic at play: lifestyle inflation disguised as "quality of life" improvements.

Living abroad often unlocks options that felt out of reach before. You might eat out more because it's affordable and enjoyable. You might travel more because everything feels closer. You might choose a nicer apartment because, compared to your US rent, it still feels like a deal.

Each of these choices makes sense on its own. Collectively, though, they can erase much of the savings you expected.

Living abroad doesn't automatically make life cheaper; it makes life more flexible. And flexibility cuts both ways. You gain access to better experiences at lower individual prices, but you also gain more opportunities to spend.

The real question isn't whether a country is cheaper on paper. It's whether the lifestyle *you're likely to build there* fits the budget you actually have.

That's why the most useful cost-of-living planning doesn't start with global rankings. It starts with a realistic picture of how *you* live, what you value, and which trade-offs you're willing to make once the novelty wears off.

SECTION 3: HOUSING, UTILITIES, AND THE ONGOING MONTHLY REALITY

In many countries, rent may *appear* lower than in major US cities, but utilities and setup costs often catch Americans off guard. It's common to receive separate bills for electricity, gas, water, trash, and sometimes even internet infrastructure. Energy prices can be volatile, and apartments may have far less insulation or climate control than US standards.

The result? You might save on rent but spend significantly more on heating a drafty apartment in winter or cooling a space without central air in summer. That's why monthly housing costs need to be evaluated as a complete package, not just a rent number pulled from a listing.

Rental terms can also operate very differently abroad. In some countries, leases are fixed term; in others, they're open-ended with strict notice requirements. You may be required to give three months' notice, find a replacement tenant, or only move out during specific windows of the year. The exit process matters just as much as the move-in.

Security deposits are another area where expectations often clash. In some countries, leaving an apartment "swept clean" is enough to recover your deposit. In others, landlords routinely deduct for minor wear and tear, making full reimbursement unlikely unless the unit is returned in perfect condition.

Housing costs abroad aren't just about what you pay each month; they're about how easy it is to enter, live in, and eventually exit a lease. Understanding those rules upfront can save you money, time, and frustration later.

"Unfurnished" May Not Mean What You Think

Another common shock is the definition of *unfurnished.*

In the United States, an unfurnished apartment usually still includes light fixtures, a built-in kitchen, and major appliances. In many countries, unfurnished means something very different, often coming as a big shock to Americans. No refrigerator. No stove. No light fixtures. Sometimes, no kitchen cabinets at all.

Germany is a well-known example. It is common for renters to purchase and install their own kitchen when they move in. That kitchen belongs to the tenant, not the landlord, and it becomes the tenant's responsibility to sell it when they move out. This has created an entire secondhand kitchen market—something that simply doesn't exist in the United States.

What looks like an affordable apartment on paper can come with high upfront costs before you've even spent your first night. Understanding local housing norms isn't optional; it's part of budgeting realistically.

Another Vote for Temporary Housing

As we noted earlier, starting with temporary and furnished housing through reputable platforms that offer payment protections and insurance can significantly reduce your exposure to housing scams. But the benefit goes beyond fraud prevention. Temporary housing gives you something far more valuable in the early months abroad: time without commitment.

Furnished apartments reduce upfront spending and logistical friction, but most importantly, they buy you breathing room: Time to learn neighborhoods instead of guessing from listings. Time to understand local rental norms, utility costs, and what "market price" actually looks like on the ground. Time to discover what unfurnished really means where you live, and whether you're prepared for it. And time to decide whether the community, city, or even the country fits your real life once the honeymoon phase fades.

SECTION 4: THE COSTS PEOPLE DON'T BUDGET FOR (BUT SHOULD)

This is where even the most organized expats get surprised.

You can meticulously budget for rent, healthcare, and groceries, and still end up feeling like your money is leaking in ways you didn't anticipate. That's because some of the most meaningful costs of expat life don't show up neatly in relocation spreadsheets. The first, and often biggest, surprise expense is the cost of traveling back to the United States. This is where even the most organized of expats get caught off guard.

Regular Travel Home

Flights back to the United States aren't always discretionary spending. Depending on where you are in life, they're how you stay connected to parents as they age, show up for young adult children navigating college, first apartments, or early careers, and remain present for births, weddings, funerals, graduations, and major family milestones. Many times, these trips are not optional luxuries; they're part of maintaining real relationships from far away.

Travel costs are also deeply tied to where you choose to live. If you expect regular trips to the United States, proximity to a major airport with direct or affordable connections should not be overlooked. A cheaper apartment three hours from a regional airport can quietly cost far more in time, stress, and airfare over the years than living closer to an international hub.

The same goes for visitors. If you hope family or friends will come see you, accessibility matters. Destinations that require multiple connections or long overland travel can reduce visits dramatically, even when people genuinely want to visit.

For those on tighter budgets, this reality can be painful. Missing family gatherings, holidays, or once-in-a-lifetime moments because flights are unaffordable is a financial and emotional trade-off. That's why it's important to be honest up front about what's realistic for your situation.

Administrative and Compliance Costs

One of the least visible, but most persistent costs of living abroad is administration.

Expat life almost always comes with ongoing compliance obligations that simply don't exist when you live in one country. Many Americans find themselves paying for tax preparation in two systems every year, even when their financial situation hasn't changed much. Add in the cost of accountants who understand cross-border rules, translators for official documents, notaries, and occasional legal advice, and the line items start adding up big time.

On top of that are the recurring fees tied to residency itself: visa renewals, permit extensions, registrations, and mandatory filings with local authorities. Each fee may feel manageable in isolation, but together they create a permanent "admin tax" on expat life, one that doesn't disappear once you're settled.

> **Expert Insight:** *When moving abroad, often the moving and settlement of personal goods, living accommodations, and migrating family tend to be the focus. However, after getting settled into life in a foreign jurisdiction, things like estate planning come into focus. One of the problems we have observed is ex-pats moving to foreign jurisdictions without many family or trusted relationships. So, when it comes to appointing a general/financial power of attorney abroad, or a trustee, the default is to appoint a family member or a trusted friend back in the United States. However, where "mind and management" of an estate takes place is where the estate is taxed. This complicates things and can lead to double tax situations because you have assets in a place like Canada (our area of expertise) but estate management now back in the United States. Same with things like guardianship of children where children are now moved from where they are settled to go back to the United States to be with trusted family members. This is a difficult issue often unforeseen when moving abroad but is worthy consideration. A good advisor should go through an estate plan design meeting to ensure these matters a thought through before going to the estate planning attorney.*
>
> *—Brian Wruk, MBA, CFP®(US), CFP®(CA), TEP, CIM, RFP®, Transition Financial Advisors*

Currency Risk and "Phantom Costs"

Currency risk is a highly underestimated cost of living abroad because it doesn't arrive as a bill.

When exchange rates move, your budget can change overnight without you spending a single extra dollar. A weakening US dollar makes rent, groceries, utilities, tuition, and travel more expensive in local terms, even though your lifestyle hasn't changed at all. A strengthening dollar can offer temporary relief, but it's unpredictable and not something you can rely on.

As I write this in early 2026, we've seen a meaningful weakening of the dollar against several major currencies. For US expats, that shift has had very real consequences. Local living costs have increased in dollar terms while long-term savings held in US accounts haven't grown to compensate. In some cases, expats paid in local currency have also found themselves unexpectedly above the Foreign Earned Income Exclusion (see Chapter 4 for a more detailed explanation about the FEIE) threshold once income is translated back into US dollars, triggering additional US tax exposure without any actual raise in income.

This is what makes currency risk so tricky: it creates "phantom costs." Your spending hasn't changed. Your income hasn't changed. But the math has.

One of the most effective ways to manage this risk is by maintaining a solid cash reserve in your local currency. This helps reduce your dependence on constant currency conversions for day-to-day life. Having several months of expenses in local currency can stabilize your cash flow during periods of volatility and prevent you from being forced to exchange money at unfavorable rates just to pay routine bills.

At the same time, expats need to balance competing forces. Holding too much cash exposes you to inflation risk, especially in higher-inflation environments. Holding too little increases liquidity risk and makes your monthly budget vulnerable to exchange rate swings. There's no perfect number, but the goal is resilience, not optimization.

Pro Tips: Building Smart Local Currency Reserves

Holding cash in your local currency is one of the simplest ways to reduce financial stress abroad. The right amount depends on your income stability and life stage. Here are some practical tips you can follow to protect yourself from the volatility of global markets:

- An individual who is employed and paid locally: Keep three to six months of expenses in local currency to smooth exchange-rate swings, job changes, and administrative delays.
- Self-employed or supporting a family: Aim for 6–12 months to account for income variability and higher fixed costs.
- Short-term goals (one to three years): Save in the currency you'll spend for major purchases like a car or home to avoid converting funds at an unfavorable exchange rate.
- Retired and living on US assets: Consider one to three years of local expenses, depending on reliable and regular income sources like Social Security or pensions, to avoid forced transfers during weak currency periods.

SECTION 5: EXPAT COST WRAP-UP CHECKLIST

You don't need to optimize every line item before you move. You *do* need to sanity-check the big categories that most expats underestimate.

Use this as a final pass before committing to your move, or as a reset if you're already abroad and feeling stretched.

Before You Move

- **Separate setup costs from lifestyle costs:** Make sure your budget clearly distinguishes one-time expenses (visas, deposits, temporary housing, furniture) from ongoing monthly spending.
- **Plan for liquidity, not just totals:** Ask: *How much cash will I need upfront, and how quickly?* Housing deposits, agency fees, and overlapping costs often require large sums at once.
- **Assume your first year will cost more than expected:** Temporary housing premiums, duplicate expenses, and learning-curve mistakes are normal, not a budgeting failure. Build in a 10–20% buffer.
- **Stress-test housing assumptions:** Factor in utilities, heating/cooling, internet setup, and what "unfurnished" actually means locally. If kitchens or appliances aren't included, price them out in advance.
- **Start with temporary housing when possible:** Budget more for flexibility and protection early to reduce scam risk and avoid locking into a long-term lease too quickly.
- **Reality-check travel expectations:** Budget for regular trips home, emergency travel, and higher holiday airfare. Consider airport access and flight routes when choosing where to live.
- **Build local-currency reserves intentionally:** Hold enough cash in local currency to cover several months of expenses so you're not forced to convert money during unfavorable exchange-rate periods. Low-cost options for doing this include services like Wise, Revolut, Interactive Brokers, or Fidelity. Review your existing banking and brokerage accounts first; you may already have this capability. Always compare fees before opening anything new.

After You Arrive

- **Track your actual spending for 6–12 months:** Your first real data set matters more than any pre-move estimate.
- **Identify what normalized and what didn't:** Which "temporary" costs disappeared? Which became permanent?
- **Rebuild buffers if they were used:** Emergency funds, moving reserves, and currency cushions often take a hit in year one. Plan to replenish them.
- **Reprice your lifestyle honestly:** Dining out, travel, private services, and convenience costs often increase, not because you're irresponsible, but because life is now different.
- **Annual budget check-in with confidence, not guilt:** Adjustments aren't a failure. They're how your expat finances stay on track. You need to know your numbers to know if your plan is sustainable.

Moving abroad isn't cheap. It *can* be cheaper, but only if you understand where your money is actually going.

The biggest financial mistakes expats make aren't about overspending. They're about underestimating transition costs and overestimating how quickly life will stabilize.

When you plan only for rent and groceries, you miss the real drivers of expat finances:

- Upfront cash demands
- Housing friction
- Travel as emotional infrastructure
- Administrative overhead
- Currency risk
- Lifestyle shifts that feel small individually but add up over time

When you plan for the full picture of expat life, especially the messy first years, moving targets, and very human priorities, you gain something far more valuable than savings: you gain resilience, confidence, and the ability to enjoy the life you're building abroad without constantly worrying about what you missed. That's not just financial planning. That's how you build a sustainable life overseas.

PART II

THE UNITED STATES FOLLOWS YOU

CHAPTER FOUR

DO I STILL HAVE TO PAY US TAXES IF I LIVE ABROAD?

The Key Question Is Really: "Do I still need to *file a US tax return* after I move abroad?"

Here's the short answer: **Yes, you do.**

Cue the collective groan.

The answer is, "It depends, but for most people, probably not, with some nuance."

This is the moment that most Americans abroad realize they didn't actually leave the IRS behind at the airport. The United States is one of only two countries in the world (the other is Eritrea) that practices *citizenship-based taxation*. Translation? If you're a US citizen or green card holder, you owe Uncle Sam a tax return every year, no matter where you live or how much tax you already paid elsewhere.

But here's the good news: while the rules are strict, the United States has built-in systems that prevent most expats from paying *double* tax on the same income. The key is understanding the rules and not falling for the myths that circulate in unregulated, heavily anecdotal spaces, such as expat Facebook groups.

FILING REQUIREMENTS FOR US CITIZENS ABROAD

Let's bust a few common myths right away.

Myth 1: "If I Move Abroad, I Don't Have to File a US Tax Return"

Wrong.

The IRS doesn't care where you live; if your income is above the filing thresholds, you're on the hook. And those thresholds aren't exactly generous: in 2026, it's $16,550 for single filers.

Here's the kicker: if you're Married Filing Separately (which many expats end up doing for practical reasons), the threshold is just $5. Yes, $5. And if you have self-employment income, the filing trigger is only $400.

Most thresholds are adjusted annually for inflation, so always check the IRS website for the latest numbers. But note: the $5 and $400 thresholds haven't budged in years.

Translation? Unless you've fully renounced your US citizenship or green card, assume you need to file every year.

> **Expert Insight:** *Many U.S. citizens do not know they must continue to file tax returns when they move abroad. People move to away from the U.S. and think they can just stop filing U.S. tax returns, but this creates*

> *noncompliance, back-taxes, penalties, and interest, and can be very stressful.*
>
> *—Lucas Wennersten CFA® CFP® (US), CFP® (CA), 49th Parallel Wealth Management*

Myth 2: "If I Earn Under $130K (2026) a Year, I Don't Have to File"

Wrong again.

That number comes from the **Foreign Earned Income Exclusion (FEIE)** (more on that in a moment). But you don't *automatically* qualify just because you earn less than the threshold. You still have to file, claim the exclusion properly, and meet the physical presence or bona fide residence tests.

Keep in mind: this FEIE limit is indexed for inflation and adjusted every year. But unlike filing thresholds, the exclusion doesn't apply automatically; you must claim it correctly, or it doesn't count.

Myth 3: "If I Pay Taxes in My New Country, I Don't Owe Anything to the United States"

Maybe. Maybe not. You still need to file a US tax return every year, and depending on your situation, you'll use either the FEIE or the Foreign Tax Credit (FTC) to reduce or eliminate double taxation.

But here's the reality check: just because these tools exist doesn't mean you're fully off the hook. US expats often face differences in **what** is taxed and **when** it's taxed. For example, a tax-free savings account abroad might be taxable in the United States, or certain deductions available locally may not apply on your US return. The result? US citizens generally end up paying the **higher of the two tax bills** either in their country of residence or to the IRS.

Myth 4: "If I Don't Tell the IRS, They Won't Know"

Most probably wrong—and a risky, potentially very expensive bet to make. Read up on FATCA and FBAR below.

FATCA AND FBAR: WHAT THEY REALLY MEAN FOR YOU

If your foreign bank has ever shut down your account or limited what types of accounts you're allowed to open, after seeing your US passport, you've already met FATCA, even if you didn't know its name.

FATCA (Foreign Account Tax Compliance Act)

Enacted in 2010 and enforced from 2014 through agreements with most other countries, this law requires foreign banks to report information about their US citizen clients to the IRS. Remember earlier, when I mentioned that opening a local foreign bank account could be tricky because some banks simply refuse to work with US clients? FATCA is why.

The original goal of this legislation was to catch billionaires hiding assets offshore, but the fallout lands squarely on everyday expats. Many banks now limit services, charge higher fees, or outright refuse to work with US citizens because the compliance burden is so heavy.

And here's the kicker: even if you hold multiple passports, your US ties always take priority in the eyes of the bank.

FBAR (Foreign Bank Account Report)

If you have more than $10,000 combined across all foreign accounts at any point during the year, you must file this separate report with the US Treasury. That $10,000 threshold has never been indexed for inflation, which means nearly every US expat with even modest savings or joint accounts hits the filing requirement each year. (Refer to Figure 4.1.)

Figure 4.1 Examples of "more than $10,000 combined across all foreign accounts."

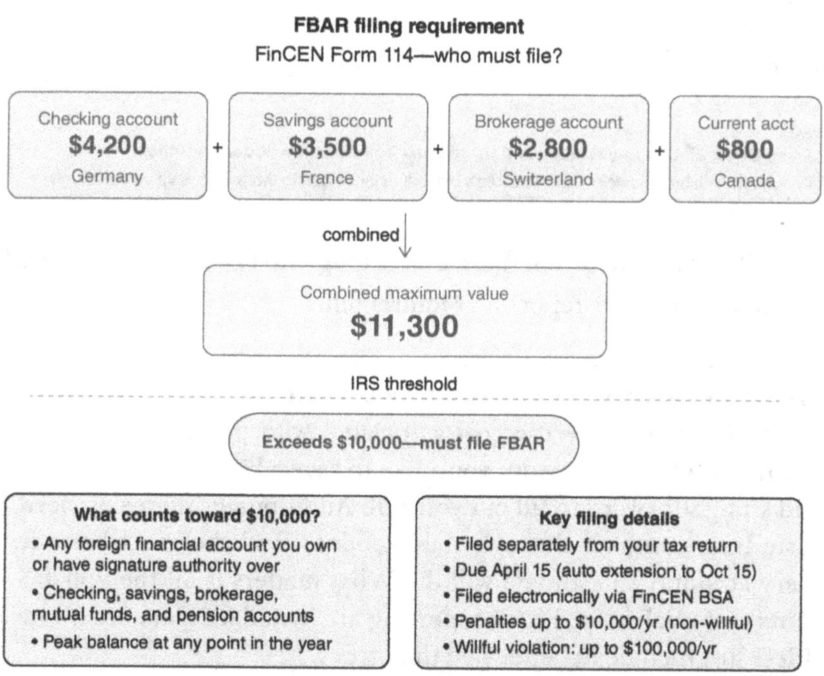

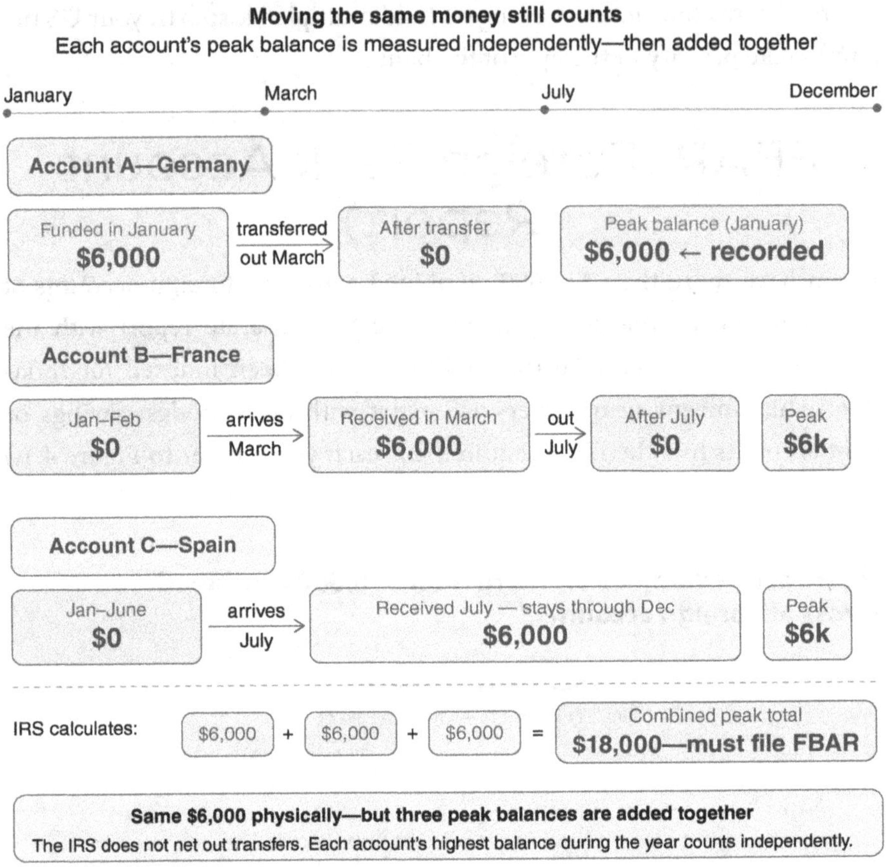

Forgetting it can lead to brutal fines, even though no tax is owed, since this is purely an information-reporting requirement.

> **Tip:** Many expat tax service providers will charge $100 or more to file this form, in addition to the cost associated with preparing your tax return. If, for whatever reason, you'd like to save a bit, this form is simple and straightforward to fill out yourself. Additionally, there's no need to waste time combing through statements to find the exact balance on every account; an estimate will do. What matters is all the non-US accounts that qualify for FBAR reporting are included. Not sure if one qualifies? Just include it; better safe than sorry.

Bottom line: FATCA makes life more complicated, and FBAR is nonnegotiable. Neither should scare you, but both should be on your annual US tax filing checklist.

EXPAT TAX PROVISIONS, TAX TREATIES, AND TOTALIZATION AGREEMENTS

Remember at the beginning, when I mentioned that while you nearly always have to file, you usually won't owe? Believe it or not, this section is where things get a little more fun because these are the tools that prevent you from being taxed twice on the same dollar. (Sorry, my tax nerd is *definitely* showing.)

- **FEIE:** This provision is claimed via IRS Form 2555. At first glance, it looks sexy and easy, allowing you exclude up to $132,900 (2026) of earned income (the exact amount changes yearly) if you meet one of two requirements: the Bona Fide Residency or Physical Presence Test. Contrary to mainstream understanding, though, this provision is typically not advisable for active earners in high-tax countries, such as France, Spain, Germany, Croatia, or Greece. The reasons are nuanced, and it's important to mention that the previous applies only where local income tax is being applied, but broadly, the FEIE is generally considered great for moderate earners in countries with lower tax rates than those in the United States.
- **FTC:** This provision is claimed via IRS Form 1116. Much more arduous to complete, it gives you a dollar-for-dollar credit for

foreign taxes you've paid. Perfect for tax residents in high-tax countries (broadly: think Europe).

- **Tax treaties:** These are agreements between the United States and specific countries to prevent double taxation and clarify which country has the right to tax certain types of income (such as pensions, Social Security, or dividends). It's important to note that each agreement is unique; the provisions of the US–France tax treaty are different from those in the US–New Zealand tax treaty, and so forth. Moreover, it's not always the case that a tax treaty exists, and they can be subject to change; on January 8, 2023, the United States terminated the double taxation treaty it had established with Hungary in 1979.
- **Totalization agreements**: Tax treaties answer the question, "Which country gets to tax this income?"; totalization agreements answer a different, but equally important question: "Which country's social security system do I pay into?"

  Totalization agreements are bilateral agreements between the United States and 30 countries designed to prevent workers from paying social security taxes to two systems on the same earnings. Without these agreements, Americans working abroad (and foreign nationals working in the United States) could be required to contribute to both systems at once, often without receiving meaningful benefits from one or the other.

  In practical terms, a totalization agreement generally ensures that you pay into only one social security system at a time, usually based on where you are working and how long you expect to stay. For example, if you are temporarily assigned abroad by a US employer, you may remain covered under the US Social Security system and be exempt from local social security contributions. Conversely, if you are working locally in another country on a longer-term basis, you may be required to contribute to that country's social insurance system instead of the US one.

Totalization agreements can also help you combine work credits from multiple countries to qualify for retirement benefits. If you don't have enough US work credits to qualify for Social Security on your own, credits earned in a totalization-agreement country may be used to help you meet eligibility thresholds (though the benefit amount is still prorated).

Most expats end up using a mix of these tools over time, depending on where they live and how much they earn. See Section 6. Practical Tax-Saving Strategies for Expats to learn more.

Expert Insight: *If you want to know whether a country can tax your income, don't just cannonball into a tax treaty article that talks about your type of income and declare victory. Treaties read less like a cookbook and more like a mystery novel, you don't start somewhere at the end of the book and expect the plot to make sense.*

The treaty article that tells you "who may tax" is not the same one that tells you "how double tax is avoided." Many treaties use an "avoidance of double taxation"/"relief from double taxation" article (often Article 23 or 24) to explain the mechanism, commonly a foreign tax credit approach. And even then, the treaty's fine print matters: The United States typically agrees to allow a credit only "in accordance with the provisions and subject to the limitations of the law of the United States." That phrase is basically the treaty saying: "Yes, relief exists... and no, it's not a free-for-all."

Other countries may start the analysis by looking at domestic law first and therefore apply internal regulations, complex residency determination rules, and long-standing court cases, which oftentimes can overturn the result of the treaty provision that you would expect when simply reading the treaty article relevant to your type of income.

(Continued)

(Continued)

> *While AI can often be great at explaining what an article of the treaty says, an international tax professional is always who you want to confirm whether an article applies to your facts and circumstances and whether both treaty countries involved can actually be trusted to consistently apply the treaty provisions they have mutually agreed to.*
>
> *—Christian Gulizzi, CPA/StB/LL.M., Gulizzi Consulting*

US FILING DEADLINES FOR EXPATS

One of the biggest traps for Americans abroad is assuming the April 15 deadline doesn't apply anymore. It does, but with a few important caveats for expats:

- **April 15:** The regular US tax return due date, and the day any tax owed must be paid. Even if you qualify for an extension to file, interest on unpaid balances starts accruing from this date. This deadline is especially critical for Americans in low- or no-tax countries (where you may not have foreign taxes to offset US liability) or for anyone with income that generates US tax due.
- **June 15:** Americans living abroad receive an automatic two-month extension to file their US tax return. But beware, this is extra time to file, not to pay. Any tax owed is still due by April 15, and interest begins accruing from then. To avoid penalties, make sure you (or your tax preparer) clearly note "Automatic Extension for Taxpayers Abroad" on your return so that the IRS processes it correctly.

- **October 15:** You can request a standard extension to file your US return by this date, but here's the key: the extension request must be filed by June 15 if you're an expat. Remember, this extension gives you more time to file, not more time to pay. Any tax due should still be paid by April 15 to avoid interest.
- **December 15:** In rare cases, expats can request a final two-month discretionary extension. Unlike the earlier deadlines, this one is not automatic; you must submit a written letter to the IRS explaining why you need the extra time. The request must be made by October 15, and approval is not guaranteed.

> **Pro Tips**
>
> - Even if you qualify for an extension, always estimate and pay your US tax liability by April 15 to avoid interest and penalties.
> - Sometimes it's easier to file every year, even if you technically don't have a filing obligation. If the IRS is used to seeing your return and suddenly doesn't, they may send you a notice, which can be more hassle than filing a simple return.

OTHER DEADLINES TO KEEP IN MIND

Federal income tax deadlines aren't the only ones US expats need to track:

- **Other IRS filings:** Forms like 3520 (foreign trusts and gifts), 5471 (foreign corporations), 8865 (foreign partnerships), and FBAR filings each have their own due dates, often tied to your regular tax return deadline. Missing them can trigger steep penalties.
- **Estimated tax payments:** The IRS expects payments throughout the year, not just at filing. If the tax you owe isn't withheld, quarterly estimated payments are due in April, June, September, and January.

- **Calendar shifts:** If a due date falls on a weekend or US federal holiday, the deadline typically moves to the next business day.
- **State taxes:** Some states may also shift deadlines for state-specific holidays, so if you're still tied to a state, double-check their calendar.

Tip: Remember, everything we've covered here is just around your US filing obligations. You'll also need to track the deadlines in your country of residence. It's important to note that not all countries follow the US calendar year. For example, the UK tax year runs from April to April, while Australia runs from July to June. Juggling two systems with different rules and timelines is part of the expat tax puzzle, so plan ahead and don't assume the deadlines or filing requirements in your new country automatically line up with US considerations. It's also worth noting that you'll likely want to complete your foreign filing before filing your US return, since the latter requires information from the foreign tax return.

You can also count on delays with processing your returns in your new country. Even in "modern" European countries (like Germany), you may not know your final tax liability for one to two years after the return was filed, which may retroactively affect your tax rate back in the United States. Amendments to the previously filed tax return or adjustments to the current one may be necessary in this case.

Expert Insight: *For anyone considering starting or investing in a business abroad, here is a lesson I learned the hard way.*

Before launching an international venture, speak with a tax expert or an experienced cross-border lawyer about your personal tax exposure. Not just the company structure, but how your ownership will be treated in each country where you are a taxpayer.

I did not do this early enough. After nearly three years running my business, I finally sought professional advice due to the increasing

> *complexity of my personal taxes. That was when I discovered that, as the primary shareholder of my company in France, I was subject to the US GILTI tax regime.*
>
> *It was not something I had planned for, and it surfaced later through my US tax filings in the form of unexpected liabilities and back taxes.*
>
> *International entrepreneurship offers extraordinary opportunities and rewards. But tax systems do not always align with the way businesses actually operate across borders. A short conversation with the right advisor (or a few) before making any plans can prevent years of complications later.*
>
> *If you are building internationally, make sure tax strategy is part of your foundation, not an afterthought.*
>
> *—Céline Flores-Tavukcuoglu, CEO of Céline Concierge*

PRACTICAL TAX-SAVING STRATEGIES FOR EXPATS

1. **Choose the right tool for your country.**

   The two most powerful tools in your US expat tax kit are the **FEIE** and the **FTC.** Which one works best depends on your situation. In high-tax countries like Europe, the FTC often makes more sense. In low- or no-tax countries like the UAE, the FEIE is usually your best bet.

   But here's what many expats miss:

   - You can't double-dip: the same income can't be shielded by both the FEIE and the FTC.

- In some cases, you may use a combination (for example, excluding part of your income under FEIE and applying FTC on the rest).
- Once you switch from FEIE to fully using the FTC, you generally can't go back to the FEIE for five years without IRS permission.
- Fully excluding your earned income with the FEIE means you'll have no "earned income" available for IRA contributions.
- Using the FEIE also makes you ineligible for the refundable Child Tax Credit, which can cost families thousands of dollars in lost benefits.

> **Pro Tip:** Choosing between the FEIE and FTC isn't just about this year's taxes; it can have ripple effects on your retirement savings and family benefits. Take the time to understand your income, tax situation, and long-term plans before locking yourself in.

2. **Know your housing benefits:** The Foreign Housing Exclusion/Deduction lets you exclude certain housing expenses if you qualify for the FEIE. This can be especially valuable in high-cost cities like London, Geneva, or Hong Kong.
3. **Don't forget Social Security:** In some countries, you may still owe US self-employment tax even if you exclude your income using the FEIE. That's where Totalization Agreements come in. These are bilateral agreements (the United States currently has them with around 30 countries) that prevent you from paying into two social security systems at once. Think of them as cousins of tax treaties, but specifically for social security.
4. **Plan for currency exchange impacts:** Fluctuations in exchange rates can create phantom taxable income (or losses) on your US return. Keep records of exchange rates on key dates (like when you were paid, when you sold property, or when you made investments).

5. **Think about retirement accounts:** Contributions to local pensions or retirement accounts may or may not be deductible in the US Tax treaties can sometimes help, but sometimes they don't. Planning ahead and speaking with a country-specific cross-border financial advisor can ensure that you don't end up double-taxed when you retire.
6. **Keep good records:** Save proof-of-residency, tax payments, and income because the IRS loves documentation. A good rule of thumb is to keep records for at least three years (the standard audit window) but hold onto them for seven years if you've claimed things like the FEIE, FTC, or have complex filings. Digital copies are fine, as long as they're clear and accessible.
7. **Mind the state tax connection:** If you still have ties to a US state, it may continue to tax you unless you formally sever residency. States like California, New Mexico, and Virginia are notorious for this. Check with your state's tax department to see what documentation is required.
8. **Plan gifts and inheritance carefully:** Inheritances received abroad may not be taxed, but they could trigger US reporting requirements (like Form 3520). On the flip side, estate tax treaties can sometimes reduce exposure.
9. **Get help when needed:** Expats often face some of the most complex tax returns in the world. Even if you don't earn a high income, your return can get messy fast if you own a business, receive equity compensation, hold foreign real estate, or juggle multiple bank accounts. In these cases, hiring a specialist isn't a luxury; it's in your long-term financial best interest. The right cross-border financial professional can keep you compliant, minimize costly mistakes, and free up your energy for building your life abroad instead of battling IRS forms.

Tip: If you are fortunate enough to be sent on an expat assignment through your US-based employer, you will typically be provided with compliance, tax preparation, and (potentially) equalization services. Keep in the back of your mind that the company hired to perform these services ultimately works for your employer, which may bias the positions that they take in their favor. They are also not being paid to take a holistic view of your financial situation or long-term plans. Experience has shown that independently hiring a second set of eyes to review your documents and lifelong goals can help you avoid costly mistakes in the long run.

QUICK CHECKLIST

- **File a US tax return every year**—even abroad, unless you've formally given up citizenship/green card.
- **Determine whether FEIE or FTC works best for you**—you can use both in limited ways, but you cannot claim both benefits on the same dollar of income, and the choice can affect things like IRA eligibility and the Child Tax Credit. Also note the "lockout" rule: if you stop using the FEIE and move to using only the FTC, you may be prevented from re-electing the FEIE for up to five years unless you obtain IRS permission. Choose carefully and make the decision with your longer-term plan in mind.
- **File an FBAR** if your combined foreign accounts exceed **$10,000** at any time during the year. This is a separate filing from your US Federal Tax Filing.
- **Check for other required forms or filing requirements** like Form 8938 (FATCA), 3520 (foreign gifts/trusts), 5471 (foreign corporations), or 8865 (foreign partnerships).

- **Review tax treaties and totalization agreements**—see if your country has one and how it applies to you.
- **Track both US and local deadlines:** they often don't line up with April 15.
- **Keep solid records:** proof of residency, foreign tax paid, and exchange rates.
- **Get professional help,** especially if you own a business, receive equity compensation, move mid-year, or hold foreign real estate. Even if your situation seems simple, it's smart to work with a professional in your first year abroad. This gives you a reliable template for future filings and ensures you don't miss new forms or requirements that come with international living. Look for a tax preparer who specializes in the expat/international space; most US tax preparers won't be equipped for these complexities.

Final Word

Moving abroad changes your lifestyle, your language, and maybe even your coffee order, but it doesn't change the fact that you must still report your financial activities to the US government.

What does change is the vocabulary. Say goodbye to familiar terms like W-2s and 401(k)s, and hello to a new alphabet soup of forms: Form 2555 (Foreign Earned Income Exclusion), Form 1116 (Foreign Tax Credit), and Form 8938 (foreign account reporting), to name just a few. (And if those don't look familiar, you glazed over and should definitely flip back and reread this chapter—no judgment, it happens!)

Learning this new financial language is part of expat life. With the right strategies, you'll stay compliant, avoid double taxation, and keep more of your money for the adventures that inspired your move abroad in the first place.

CHAPTER FIVE

WHAT HAPPENS TO MY US RETIREMENT ACCOUNTS ABROAD?

Key Question: What happens to my US retirement accounts if I move abroad, and do I need to do anything right away?

Moving abroad doesn't mean starting over when it comes to retirement, but it does mean playing by a new set of rules. Your existing US retirement accounts don't disappear when you cross a border. A 401(k) doesn't self-destruct at passport control. Your IRA doesn't care what country you sleep in at night. From a purely mechanical standpoint, those accounts can stay exactly where they are.

Where expats get tripped up isn't in what exists, but in what changes once you're living outside the United States. Many assume they can keep doing exactly what they've always done, just from a different country. Others assume retirement planning should be put on hold entirely until they "figure out where they'll end up," so they press pause for years. Both approaches can be costly. Missed contribution years, poorly timed rollovers, misunderstood tax treatment, and irreversible decisions made too early can erode long-term security.

The reality sits somewhere in between. Retirement planning absolutely still matters abroad. It just requires a more intentional, globally informed approach, one that prioritizes flexibility and coordination over optimization.

This chapter will help you understand the following:

- What stays the same when you move abroad
- What changes, sometimes subtly and sometimes dramatically
- Why doing nothing is often safer than doing the "wrong something" too soon

DO I NEED TO DO ANYTHING WITH MY US RETIREMENT ACCOUNTS RIGHT NOW?

When it comes to US retirement accounts, the right move depends on both what you do and when you do it.

If you're still in the exploratory phase, testing countries, on a temporary assignment, or genuinely unsure where you'll land long term, doing nothing can be the most strategic choice. Leaving your US retirement accounts exactly as they are preserves flexibility while your plans are still in motion and avoids triggering tax consequences in a country you may not stay in.

But once you establish tax residency abroad, the calculus changes.

After residency is established, your new country often gains taxing rights over your US retirement accounts. At that point, many of the most valuable planning opportunities are either limited or gone entirely. Decisions that would have been neutral or even advantageous before the move, such as rollovers, Roth conversions, or restructuring accounts, can suddenly carry real foreign tax costs. This is why pre-move and pre-residency planning matters so much.

In higher-tax countries, there may be a narrow window before residency begins to accomplish the following:

- Consolidate or roll over accounts while they're still treated cleanly.
- Execute Roth IRA contributions or conversions while those accounts are more likely to be respected or taxed favorably.
- Reduce future reporting friction or exposure to annual foreign taxation.

In lower-tax or territorial tax systems, the opposite may be true. Holding off on changes can be intentional. If you're leaving a high-tax US state or moving to a jurisdiction with lower effective tax rates, your combined tax burden may improve *after* the move, making it sensible to delay taxable actions until residency shifts.

The takeaway isn't "act fast" or "do nothing."

It's this: Know where you are in your relocation journey and align your retirement decisions to that timing.

Exploring? Preserve flexibility. Committing long-term? Understand, in detail, how your new country will tax your US retirement accounts before residency begins.

Once residency is established, planning is still possible, but many of the most efficient, pre-residency strategies are no longer available.

That's why I can't overstate the value of engaging a cross-border professional before you arrive, even if it's just for a single hour. A good advisor will ask questions you didn't know to ask, flag issues you didn't realize existed, and help you see decisions that carry long-term consequences well beyond your first year abroad.

In my own practice, I've seen thoughtful pre-move planning save clients hundreds of thousands of dollars in avoidable taxes, and in some cases, shape planning outcomes that affect tens of millions over a lifetime. Those opportunities rarely come from doing something complicated. They come from doing the right things at the right time.

Employer-sponsored Plans: 401(k), 403(b), and 457 Plans

For many US expats, an old 401(k), 403(b), or 457 plan becomes a "legacy" account after a move abroad. The account itself doesn't disappear, but how usable, flexible, and efficient it is can change in ways people don't anticipate.

Access and Account Management Issues

One of the first surprises expats encounter is that not all plan providers are comfortable servicing accounts with foreign addresses, even if you are a US citizen. Some providers restrict trading, limit rebalancing, or move accounts into what's effectively a "maintenance-only" mode, where you can log in and view balances, but you can't easily make changes.

Administrative friction is also common. Two-factor authentication tied to US phone numbers, mailed paperwork sent to old addresses, and limited customer support for non-US residents can turn routine account management into a recurring hassle. None of this is catastrophic, but it does increase the odds that the account becomes "out of sight, out of mind" rather than money that is intentionally working *for* you.

Tax and Regulatory Considerations

From a tax perspective, employer-sponsored plans continue to follow US rules, but your resident country may layer its own interpretation on top. If you take distributions while living abroad, you may find your custodian requires mandatory withholding regardless of whether you will actually owe tax due to your foreign address.

You cannot make new contributions to a former employer's plan, which means the account becomes a static asset over time. Depending on your most recent US state of residence, state tax exposure may persist if domicile was never formally severed.

> **Pro Tip**
>
> - Retirement accounts tied to US employment can carry very different tax consequences for the non-US spouse. If a non-US person takes distributions from a US retirement account (such as a 401(k)), the IRS generally requires 30% mandatory federal withholding, unless a tax treaty between the US and the country of residence provides a reduced rate. Even when treaty relief applies, the country where you live may still tax the withdrawal, sometimes without offering a full credit for the US tax already withheld.

If you or your spouse is not a US citizen, distributions from US retirement accounts should always be reviewed in advance with a cross-border professional. A small planning step here can prevent large, avoidable tax surprises later.

Investment, Currency, and Fee Friction

Most employer-sponsored US retirement plans (401(k), 403(b), 457, etc.) offer a limited investment menu designed for US-based employees. Once you're living abroad, those options may no longer align with your global strategy, currency needs, or risk tolerance.

Because the account is denominated in US dollars, currency risk becomes more visible. If your future spending will be in euros, francs, or another currency, exchange-rate movements can erode purchasing power, even if your account balance looks healthy in USD terms.

Fees are another overlooked issue. Some employers pass on higher administrative costs to former employees, which can erode returns over time without much visibility.

Estate and Administrative Risks

Legacy accounts are easy to forget, especially if you've moved countries, changed names, or shifted financial institutions. Over time, this increases the risk of missed planning opportunities or poor beneficiary coordination. If your beneficiary is a non-US citizen, additional tax and legal complexity may arise for your heirs. And in certain cases, employers are legally allowed to force small balances into IRAs of their choosing, or even cash them out, if balances fall below specific thresholds.

So, Should You Leave It, Roll It, or Cash Out?

For many expats, leaving a solid, low-cost 401(k), or other US retirement plan, where it is, at least initially, is a perfectly reasonable choice. It avoids triggering immediate US tax consequences, preserves tax-deferred growth, and maintains strong creditor protections.

That said, this is not a one-size-fits-all rule. How a 401(k) should be handled depends heavily on where you're moving, how long you expect to stay, and how your new country taxes US retirement accounts. The real risk isn't leaving the account alone in the early stages; it's leaving it untouched indefinitely, without ever reassessing whether it still fits your cross-border life.

What about cashing out?

Yes, it is technically possible to cash out a 401(k) when you leave the United States. But for the vast majority of people, who are not in retirement, it's one of the most damaging financial decisions they can make during an international move.

Early distributions often trigger a cascade of consequences all at once: immediate US income tax, a potential 10% early withdrawal penalty, possible taxation in your new country of residence, and the permanent loss of decades of tax-advantaged compounding. What can feel like a clean break or a way to simplify during an already stressful transition is, in reality, an extremely expensive shortcut.

Unless you're facing a genuine financial emergency, cashing out a retirement account should be viewed as a last resort. In cross-border planning, the goal is flexibility and optionality. Cashing out permanently closes doors you may wish you had kept open later.

Before you move and establish tax residency in a new country, it's essential to understand how that country treats US employer-sponsored plans versus IRAs. Many of the most efficient planning opportunities exist before residency begins, and once that window closes, they can be difficult or impossible to recreate. Taking the time to review your options with a qualified cross-border professional in this pre-move phase can help you avoid missed opportunities and prevent costly surprises later on.

Expert Insight: *Many times, a Canadian investment manager wants to use "60j" of the Canadian Income Tax Act to roll a US IRA into a Canadian RRSP under their management. 60j has some specifics qualifications related to it, but in short, it allows a withdrawal of an IRA (fully taxable in both Canada and the United States), but the taxpayer gets to claim an offsetting deduction if those same funds are contributed to an RRSP. There are a couple of problems the uninitiated run into:*

(Continued)

(Continued)

1. *The person is a US citizen or taxpayer living in Canada. In this case, the entire amount of the IRA withdrawal is subject to tax in the United States (and a 10% early penalty if withdrawing before the age of 59 1/2), which can lead to an unintended large tax bill.*
2. *The person is NOT a US taxpayer. In this case, the Canada/US Tax Treaty comes into play, and a 15% withholding is held at source from the IRA.*

With the tax withholding by the United States, the Canadian resident no longer has the full amount of the IRA withdrawal to contribute to the RRSP. Unless the Canadian resident can make it up somehow with other available cash, a portion of the tax (and early penalty) will also be fully taxable in Canada. A foreign tax credit will be allowed in Canada, but this is a simple "oops" and "ah ha" moment to consider. Further, the client has a lost opportunity cost for taxes paid earlier than required.

—Brian Wruk, MBA, CFP®(US), CFP®(Canada), TEP, CIM, RFP® of Transition Financial Advisors

IRAs ABROAD

Unlike employer-sponsored plans, IRAs are fully portable. They stay with you no matter where you live or work, and at first glance, that portability feels reassuring. You don't have to move them, close them, or replace them just because you crossed a border.

Traditional IRAs: Familiar in the United States, Inconsistent Abroad

From a US perspective, the rules are straightforward. Growth inside a Traditional IRA is tax-deferred, withdrawals are taxed as ordinary income, and required minimum distributions currently begin at age 75 (under the SECURE 2.0 Act).

It's also worth clarifying terminology here. A *Rollover IRA* and a *Traditional IRA* are treated exactly the same under US tax law. The "rollover" label simply describes how the account was funded, typically with assets moved from a former employer's 401(k) or similar plan. For US tax purposes, there is no difference in how a Rollover IRA and a Traditional IRA are taxed.

Other countries don't automatically recognize the US concept of tax deferral, and they generally don't care how an IRA was funded. Whether the account originated from a rollover or direct contributions, your resident country may tax annual growth inside the account, ignore the US deferral entirely, or apply its own rules to withdrawals that don't align with US timing or tax rates.

When the two systems aren't coordinated, you can end up paying tax sooner than expected, being taxed twice on the same income, or facing effective tax rates that exceed what you would have paid under US federal ordinary income rates.

None of this means a Traditional (or Rollover) IRA is "bad" abroad. But it does mean it can't be treated as a set-it-and-forget-it account once you're living under a second tax system. The label on the account may feel important in the United States, but abroad, what matters is how the account is classified and taxed where you live now, and where you expect to live and retire in the future.

Roth IRAs: Powerful Tool, Wrong Country = Disaster

As a US citizen, I love Roth IRAs. For millions of US taxpayers, they are one of the most generous and powerful planning tools available: contribute after-tax dollars, let the money grow, and withdraw it tax-free in retirement. It's hard to beat. The problem is that this elegant, "tax-free forever" concept is almost uniquely American. Once you move abroad, it rarely translates cleanly. Roth IRAs remain one of the most powerful retirement tools under US law, but they are also one of the easiest to misuse once you live outside the United States.

In the right country, a Roth can work exactly as intended: tax-free growth in the United States and tax-free withdrawals in retirement. That outcome typically depends on one of two things. Either a tax treaty explicitly (or implicitly) recognizes US retirement accounts, or the country operates under a territorial tax system that generally excludes foreign investment income from local taxation.

Countries like the United Kingdom, France, and Malta, as well as territorial systems such as Panama, Costa Rica, or Singapore, are places where Roth IRAs may receive favorable treatment. "May" is doing a lot of work here. Even in countries where Roths can work well, the outcome may not be automatic. Local treatment often depends on factors such as how long you've been resident, whether treaty positions are properly disclosed, how the account is classified under local law, and how income inside the Roth is characterized (dividends versus capital gains, for example). Two expats living in the same country can end up with very different results based on timing and structure alone.

For US expats, it's important to understand that Roth IRAs working as intended outside the United States is the exception, not the norm. In most countries, Roth IRAs are not recognized as special tax-exempt retirement accounts under local law. Foreign tax authorities often treat a Roth IRA as an ordinary foreign investment account. In practice, that can mean the following:

- Annual taxation of dividends and interest, even if nothing is withdrawn
- Taxation of capital gains as they accrue or are realized rather than being sheltered inside the account
- Taxation of withdrawals, despite those same distributions being completely tax-free under US law

All of that said, Roth IRAs are not automatically a lost cause for Americans abroad. When used intentionally, they can still be powerful planning tools. The key is understanding *where* and *when* they work and adjusting strategy accordingly.

First, location matters. Some countries do recognize Roth IRAs or effectively respect their tax-free treatment, either through tax treaties or territorial tax systems. In those jurisdictions, Roth contributions or conversions made before or during residency can be incredibly attractive, allowing you to "supercharge" tax-free growth in a way that works on both sides of the border. This is one of the clearest examples of why destination-driven planning matters.

Second, even in countries that do not recognize Roth treatment, there may still be strategic options. Many foreign jurisdictions tax Roth IRAs as ordinary investment accounts, but the US ordering rules still apply. That means your contributions can always be withdrawn tax- and penalty-free under US law, regardless of age. For individuals under age 59½, this opens the door to pulling out contributions before establishing foreign tax residency, reducing future exposure to local taxation.

Finally, asset allocation inside the Roth IRA matters just as much as whether the account itself is recognized.

In countries that do not fully respect Roth treatment, the local tax authority often looks through the account and taxes what's happening inside it, interest, dividends, and sometimes capital gains. That means you're not powerless, even if the Roth itself isn't protected. By being intentional about what you hold inside the Roth, you may be able to reduce or control the type of income your resident country taxes. For example, in jurisdictions that tax interest and dividends annually but treat unrealized capital gains more favorably, a Roth invested primarily in growth-oriented assets may create less current tax friction than one filled with income-producing holdings. Conversely, loading a Roth with high-dividend or interest-heavy investments can quietly trigger recurring local tax bills that undermine the account's long-term US tax advantages.

If you are already at retirement age, the planning lens shifts again. In that case, the question becomes how and where Roth distributions will ultimately be taxed and whether timing withdrawals before or after a move produces a better combined outcome.

Roth IRAs aren't universally good or bad once you live abroad. Their value depends on timing, jurisdiction, visa/tax status, and, most importantly, coordination. Getting this right requires aligning US tax rules with the laws of your resident country, which is why meaningful Roth planning should involve a qualified cross-border professional. With thoughtful, pre-residency planning, Roth IRAs can still play a powerful role in a global retirement strategy.

Investment Restrictions Inside Retirement Accounts

Even when your retirement accounts stay open, what you're allowed to invest in inside those accounts can change the moment you become a non-US resident. This is one of the more frustrating surprises expats encounter, often months or years after the move, not at the outset.

Many expats eventually discover that their investment menu has quietly narrowed. They may be able to hold existing funds but are blocked from buying more. Exchange-traded funds might still be available, while mutual funds are no longer accessible. Some custodians restrict trading unless you work through an advisor, and in certain cases entire asset classes are simply off-limits.

These limitations usually aren't personal. They arise from a combination of US custodian compliance rules and local regulations in your country of residence, such as MiFID II in the European Union, which restricts how certain investment products can be offered to retail investors.

This is why thoughtful simplification before a move can be so valuable. Many expats proactively shift their retirement accounts into broadly diversified, low-cost investments that are widely supported by expat-friendly custodians. By choosing investments you're likely to retain access to long term, you lower the risk of being locked into a portfolio you can't rebalance, adjust, or manage as your life abroad evolves.

Asset Location Gets More Complicated Abroad

Asset location is the strategy of deciding which investments belong in which types of accounts, taxable, tax-deferred, and tax-free, in order to manage taxes over time. In a purely US-based financial plan, asset location is fairly clean. Tax-inefficient assets tend to live in tax-deferred retirement accounts, growth assets go where they'll be taxed more favorably, and the rules are at least internally consistent.

Once you live abroad, that simplicity disappears.

As an expat, every asset now lives under **two tax systems at once:**

- How the US government taxes the account and the investments inside it
- How does your country of residence tax the same account and income

A strategy that looks elegant on a US tax return can become inefficient, or even punitive, once your resident country weighs in. Bonds that make sense inside an IRA may be taxed annually abroad. A Roth IRA that's tax-free in the United States may generate taxable income locally. Even the same investment can be treated differently, depending on which account holds it.

Preserve Flexibility First, Optimize Later

When it comes to US retirement accounts abroad, the most important decision is how to coordinate them.

Before making any changes, step back and ask the questions that actually matter:

- How does my current country tax this account today?
- How might that treatment change if I stay long term or move again?
- Does this decision preserve flexibility for future withdrawals, timing, and location?

When you're unsure, avoid irreversible moves. You can almost always roll a 401(k) into an IRA later. You can't undo a taxable distribution once it's taken, and you can't rewind planning opportunities that disappear after residency is established.

Doing nothing doesn't mean doing nothing thoughtfully. It doesn't mean parking everything in cash or ignoring your accounts. Often, the best interim strategy is staying invested in a simple, diversified allocation you're comfortable holding while you gain clarity about where you're going and how long you'll be there.

Your US retirement accounts are allowed to stay exactly where they are when you move abroad. Whether they should depends on far more than US rules alone.

In the next chapter, we'll turn to the system you've just entered: foreign retirement plans, an overview of the tax traps and opportunities, what these systems assume about your future, and how to coordinate them with your existing US accounts so that you can keep saving for retirement abroad in a way that actually supports the life you're building.

Expert Insight: *You might be surprised at how differently your new country can tax "familiar" US financial assets. Retirement accounts are often caught in the crosshairs, because what the United States treats as a tax-deferred retirement wrapper may be viewed abroad as something much more ordinary—and taxed accordingly. In Sweden, under current law and administrative practice as of 2026, US IRAs are generally treated as ordinary investment accounts for Swedish tax purposes, meaning Sweden does not recognize the IRA's US tax-deferred nature.*

The practical consequence is a timing mismatch: investment returns generated inside the IRA— dividends, interest, and capital gains—are taxable in Sweden as capital income when they arise under Swedish tax principles, even though the United States generally taxes IRAs primarily upon withdrawal. So, the "surprise" isn't just that tax applies—it's when: Swedish residents find themselves paying annual Swedish tax on investment income generated inside an account they assumed would be taxed only gradually in retirement. Under current rules, dividends and capital gains on listed securities are generally taxed at 30% in the Swedish capital-income category—which can be a brutal wake-up call for people who thought they were simply letting their retirement savings compound tax-deferred until retirement.

—Lori Nitzel, EA, J.D., LL.M.

PART III

INVESTING AS A US EXPAT

CHAPTER SIX

HOW DO I NAVIGATE A NEW RETIREMENT SYSTEM ABROAD?

Key Question: How do foreign pension systems fit into my retirement plan, and how do I coordinate them with my US accounts across borders?

When you move abroad, you don't just change countries. You enter an entirely new retirement and financial system, often without fully realizing it. You start a new job. Contributions are withheld automatically. Your employer mentions something about a "mandatory pension" or "social insurance," and you nod along, assuming this is just the local version of a 401(k). It isn't.

Foreign pension systems are built on very different assumptions from US retirement accounts, and they vary widely from country to country.

Some are generous, others restrictive. Some are mandatory, others are optional. Some work beautifully for US expats, while others create tax friction, reporting headaches, or liquidity problems if they're misunderstood.

This chapter can't cover every country, account type, or edge case, and it's not meant to. Instead, the goal is to give you a practical framework: an overview of the types of foreign retirement systems you're likely to encounter, the assumptions they make about your future, and a playbook for asking the right questions. With that foundation, you'll be better equipped to optimize your financial situation as a US expat while avoiding the most common and costly mistakes Americans make when navigating retirement systems abroad.

FOREIGN PENSION SYSTEMS ARE BUILT FOR LOCALS, NOT NOMADS

Most foreign pension systems are designed around one core assumption: you will live, work, and retire in the same country. That assumption works well for locals, and for most non-US expats because nearly every country in the world taxes based on residence. Once you leave, your tax ties usually end. The United States is the exception.

As a US citizen, you remain financially tied to the US tax system for life, regardless of where you live. That's why US expats can't simply follow standard local advice or even broad "expat" guidance. The tax incentives, deductions, and retirement strategies that work beautifully for locals, or for non-US expats, often don't translate cleanly once US rules are layered on top.

As a US expat, you may

- work in multiple countries over your career,
- contribute to several different pension systems,
- retire in a country that is not where you earned your pension, or
- continue filing US tax returns for life.

None of this makes foreign pensions "bad." But it does mean they require more coordination than most people expect. What feels like a simple payroll deduction today can quietly turn into a complex planning issue years later, especially once withdrawals, currency, and taxation across two systems come into play.

Expert Insight: *Most Americans who are considering the tax implications of moving abroad will reach out to a US tax expert first. However, in many cross-border situations, the local taxes are really the first piece of the puzzle to figure out. US taxes for expats fit on top of and around the local tax situation. It's important to first understand how different types of income, assets, or business structures are going to be treated in country you're moving to before moving abroad so that you can make any necessary adjustments before you become a tax resident of that country. Or at a minimum, so that you know what you're getting into and aren't surprised later. Once you have an understanding of the local tax situation, then a US tax expert can take a look at how to optimize the US taxes around the local taxes.*

—Emily Haines, CPA, Xpatax Solutions

Most Countries Use a Three-pillar Retirement System

While the details vary by country, many foreign retirement systems are built around a familiar structure, one that isn't all that different from the US model. Broadly speaking, they rely on three pillars:

Pillar One: Mandatory Social Security–style Contributions

This is the foundation of most systems. Employees (and often employers) are required to contribute to a government-run social insurance program that provides a baseline retirement benefit. Think of this as the local equivalent of US Social Security.

For US expats, this is where Totalization Agreements come back into play. These agreements, currently in place between the US and around 30 countries, are designed to prevent you from paying into two social security systems on the same earnings. Depending on your situation, they may allow you to remain in the US system or shift fully into the local one, but they don't eliminate the need to understand how benefits will ultimately be calculated and paid.

Pillar Two: Employer-sponsored Retirement Plans

The second pillar usually consists of employer-sponsored plans, often mandatory or heavily encouraged. These plans are typically tax-incentivized locally and may include employer contributions, automatic enrollment, or required participation based on income level or job type.

From a local perspective, these plans often look like an obvious "yes." From a US perspective, the answer is more nuanced. Some employer plans are protected or partially recognized under US tax treaties. Others are not. In some cases, contributions are tax-deferred locally but currently taxable in the United States or vice versa. The treaty, if one exists, matters a lot here.

Pillar Three: Personal Retirement Savings

The third pillar is where individuals save on their own through personal retirement accounts, investment wrappers, or insurance-based savings products. This is also where US expats tend to run into the most trouble.

Many of these accounts are highly tax-advantaged locally, but they often receive little or no favorable treatment under US tax law. Some are taxed currently, others trigger complex reporting, and many hold investments that are classified as passive foreign investment companies (PFICs), leading to punitive US tax outcomes. What looks like a smart, responsible savings move in your new country can quietly become one of the least efficient ways for a US expat to save.

Understanding which pillar you're contributing to, and how each one is treated under both tax systems, is essential. This is where well-meaning "water cooler" advice, applying US rules to foreign systems, or relying solely on local experts can easily trip up US expats. What works perfectly for locals, or even for other non-US expats, doesn't automatically work when you're still tied to the US tax system.

> **Expert Insight:** *In general, if you have assets you want to protect, talk to a tax specialist in the country you are moving to, before you start making "standard" financial moves based on your home-country rules. To give an example of why this matters: in Sweden, the Supreme Administrative Court held that 401(k) rollovers to IRAs by Swedish tax residents are fully taxable at the time of the rollover. In the Court's view, the timing of taxation is determined under Swedish rules without regard to when the income would be taxed under US law, and the rollover is treated as the individual having realized pension income at that moment.*
>
> *—Lori Nitzel, EA, J.D., LL.M.*

DON'T FORGET ANNUAL US TAX REPORTING

Even when no tax is due today, foreign pensions often come with ongoing US reporting obligations.

Depending on the country and structure, these may include the following:

- Foreign Bank and Financial Account Report (FBAR)
- Foreign Account Tax Compliance Act (FATCA) (Form 8938)
- Additional disclosures for foreign trust-like arrangements

Each required form adds time, complexity, and often professional fees. This is what I think of as the hidden expense ratio of foreign pensions. It never appears on an account statement, but it absolutely impacts your real, after-tax outcome. A pension that looks efficient locally can become expensive once US compliance costs are factored in. That doesn't mean it's not worth participating; it just means those costs should be acknowledged as part of the decision-making process.

TAX TREATIES AND TOTALIZATION AGREEMENTS: HELPFUL, BUT LIMITED

Tax treaties and totalization agreements come up frequently when discussing foreign pensions and, really, every aspect of life as a US expat, for good reason. When used correctly, they can be powerful tools in cross-border planning.

At their best, they may

- reduce or prevent double taxation of pension income,
- clarify which country has the primary right to tax distributions, and
- coordinate social security systems so work credits earned in multiple countries can count toward eligibility.

But this is also where many US expats get tripped up. Tax treaties are not a free pass, and they do not override the US tax system for US citizens. Unfortunately.

Almost every US income tax treaty includes what's known as a Savings Clause. While the wording may vary slightly by country, the message is remarkably consistent. For example, the US–Switzerland Income Tax Treaty states:

> Notwithstanding any provision of this Convention except paragraph 3 of this Article, the United States may tax a person who is treated as a resident under its taxation laws ... and its citizens (including its former citizens) as if this Convention had not come into effect.

In plain English, the Savings Clause means this: Ignore most of the treaty. The United States always reserves the right to tax its own citizens and tax residents as if the treaty didn't exist.

There *are* limited carve-outs, often for items like Social Security, certain government pensions, or specific treaty articles, but those exceptions are narrow and highly technical.

The practical takeaway is critical: tax treaties often work far better for non-US persons than they do for US citizens. Advice that is perfectly valid for a local citizen, or even for a non-US expat, can fall apart entirely once US citizenship-based taxation enters the picture.

This is why US expats cannot rely on "standard" local advice, or even generalized expat advice, when it comes to pensions, retirement planning, or tax incentives. Every benefit must be evaluated twice: once under your country of residence's rules and again under the US tax system. Only where those two systems align do you get a true planning opportunity.

A pension structure that is tax-advantaged, simple, and efficient for locals or other foreign nationals may lose much of its benefit once the US layer is applied. In some cases, the treaty helps only at distribution, not during the accumulation years. In others, it protects employer pensions but not personal retirement accounts. And totalization agreements, while extremely helpful, address *social security contributions*, not investment taxation or US reporting obligations.

For US expats, the question is never just, "Is this pension tax-advantaged or mandatory?" It's always: "How does this work under my local system **and** the US system, over time?"

That coordination, rather than blind reliance on treaties, is what keeps foreign pensions from becoming expensive surprises later.

HOW FOREIGN PENSIONS FIT INTO A REAL EXPAT RETIREMENT PLAN

The most productive way to think about a foreign pension isn't as *good* or *bad*. It's as **one component of a broader retirement strategy**, one that now must work across borders.

Understand the key structural reality upfront:

- **US retirement accounts cannot be rolled into foreign pension systems.**
- **Foreign pensions, even "qualified" or mandatory ones, never roll into US accounts.**

They exist in parallel. Always. That means moving abroad doesn't simplify your retirement planning; it adds a second (or third) system that must be coordinated, not merged.

Because of that, the wrong question is often: "Is this pension worth it?" There are better questions:

- How does this pension interact with my existing US retirement accounts?
- How will it be taxed by *both* countries over time, not just today?
- What currency will it ultimately pay out in, and where will I be spending?
- How flexible is it if my plans change, or if I move again?

When you ask better questions, the strategy usually becomes clearer.

> **Expert Insight:** *You need to stay engaged and run your own numbers. Where you've worked, for how long, and where you plan to live in the future all shape a retirement outcome that is uniquely yours.*
>
> *In my work with US expats living in or moving to Switzerland, many are surprised to learn that Swiss social security requires higher contributions, with no income cap like in the United States, while offering roughly half the maximum benefit.*
>
> *Not all social security systems are created equal. And while this is only one piece of your retirement plan, it's one that deserves careful attention before you rely on it.*
>
> *—Arielle Tucker, CFP®, EA*

THE MOST COMMON MISTAKE: PLANNING IN SILOS

One of the biggest mistakes US expats make isn't choosing the "wrong" pension or account. It's assuming that any one professional sees the full picture.

- Your **US accountant** understands IRS rules.
- Your **local accountant** understands your resident country's system.
- A **cross-border planner** understands how those systems interact over decades.

Most professionals don't do it all, and that's okay. What matters is **coordination.**

Even within the same country, outcomes can vary dramatically based on the following:

- Visa type
- Length of intended stay
- Employment status
- Whether your move is temporary, long term, or still evolving

High-level advice breaks down quickly at the individual level. That's why expat retirement planning is never one-size-fits-all.

A PRACTICAL CHECKLIST: QUESTIONS TO ASK BEFORE (OR WHILE) YOU CONTRIBUTE

Whether you're researching on your own or working with professionals, these are the questions that matter.

Questions to Ask Yourself

- Is this pension mandatory, optional, or avoidable?
- What assumptions does this system make about where I'll retire?

- Will I be relying on this income, or is it a supplement?
- If this is my only local retirement benefit, what gaps do I need to fill myself?

Questions for Your Local (Non-US) Accountant

- How is this pension taxed locally during accumulation and at withdrawal?
- What happens if I leave the country before retirement?
- What currency will benefits be paid in?
- Are there penalties or restrictions on early or partial withdrawals?

Questions for Your US Expat Tax Accountant

- Is growth inside this pension taxable annually in the United States?
- What US reporting applies (FBAR, Form 8938, foreign trust reporting)?
- Does a tax treaty help, and where does the savings clause limit it?
- How are distributions taxed under US rules?

Questions for a Cross-border Advisor

- How does this pension fit alongside my US or other country retirement accounts and plans?
- Where should additional retirement savings live for flexibility?
- How does currency exposure affect my long-term plan?
- What decisions today could limit my options if I move again?

CHAPTER SEVEN

HOW DO I INVEST AND MANAGE MY PORTFOLIO WHILE LIVING ABROAD?

Key Question: Can I still invest in US stocks and funds—and how do I manage my investments across borders as an expat?

When you pack your bags and move abroad, you might assume your investments can just come along for the ride. After all, money is global, right? Not exactly.

The reality is that while your dollars may cross borders easily, your access to certain investment accounts might not. Suddenly, the online brokerage you've used for years could tell you: "Sorry, we can't service your account now that you live outside the United States."

That doesn't mean you're locked out of investing; it just means you need to approach it strategically. This chapter is your roadmap to keeping your portfolio alive and well while you're overseas.

MAINTAINING ACCESS TO US BROKERAGE ACCOUNTS

The first big hurdle for expats is simply **keeping their US accounts open**. Some brokerages freeze or close accounts when you change your address to a foreign country, citing compliance headaches.

- **The good news:** Firms like Charles Schwab and Interactive Brokers generally allow expats to maintain accounts, though the rules can vary depending on your country of residence. If you work with another custodian or financial firm, confirm your situation directly; policies aren't always clear, and surprises happen. Custodians often weigh factors such as your new country of residence, the length of your account's open status, and the overall account value when deciding whether to allow you to keep it.
- **The bad news:** You may be restricted from trading certain products (like US-based mutual funds or exchange-traded funds [ETFs]) once you're overseas. Some brokers will let you *hold* but not *buy more*.

Pro Tips

- If you're planning your move, open and fund your accounts *before you leave*. It's much easier to maintain accounts abroad than to open new ones from overseas. Some account types are even tied to state law, like 529 college savings plans or custodial accounts. Even if a custodian supports expats generally, it doesn't mean you'll still have access to open new specialized accounts once you've left.

- Long before you move, broach the conversation in the hypothetical with your bank. Using language such as, "I'm thinking about spending some time abroad," and explaining that you haven't made any decisions yet while that's still the case can help you get clear, helpful answers from your banker that inform your decision-making rather than aggravate your to-do list

DON'T RUSH TO CUT ALL US FINANCIAL TIES

As we mentioned in Chapter 1, don't be too quick to close all your US financial ties. Moving abroad, especially nowadays, is often an emotionally driven process, and that can lead one to think that the best decision is to simply cut all ties. But when it comes to finances, focusing on the fundamentals always wins out: step back, assess holistically, and don't make any rash decisions. (I know, I know, much easier said than done.)

So, if you shouldn't cut financial ties, what should you do?

In your first year or two overseas, it's wise to keep things stable. When possible, maintain an intentionally curated set of US bank and brokerage accounts, keep a US mailing address, and don't rush into shutting everything down. Many US expats test the waters abroad before deciding whether it's a short-term adventure or a permanent move, and even if your intent is to move abroad permanently, there's an ongoing argument for keeping your US accounts open and funded.

Once you've committed to building your life abroad, that's the time to **update your financial institutions**, close accounts you no longer need, deepen local banking relationships, and restructure your assets with a cross-border perspective.

Example Case Study

Isabella moved to Spain and, eager to simplify, closed all her US bank accounts within the first six months. A year later, she decided the expat life wasn't for her. Reopening US accounts after living abroad proved frustrating and time-consuming; delays in getting a mortgage approval when she returned cost her the apartment she wanted.

By contrast, James moved to Singapore but kept his US accounts active during his first few years abroad. When he eventually decided to stay long term, he had the flexibility to gradually transition his finances abroad without losing his US safety net.

WHY YOU SHOULD UPDATE YOUR ADDRESS WITH FOREIGN FINANCIAL INSTITUTIONS

When you open accounts abroad, whether it's a checking account, brokerage, or even insurance, you'll be asked for a residential address. It may be tempting to keep using your US address for convenience, but keeping your information outdated can create bigger headaches down the line.

Here's why you should update your address:

- **Compliance matters:** Banks are required to know where their clients actually live (this is part of global anti-money laundering and tax compliance rules). If they discover you've provided an old or inaccurate address, they could freeze or even close your account.

- **FATCA reporting:** Under FATCA, foreign banks must report US clients' accounts to the IRS. Having the correct address ensures your records are consistent and avoids unnecessary red flags.
- **Receiving correspondence:** From tax forms to account notices, you want important documents delivered where you actually live, not sitting in a US mailbox you rarely check. Forwarding mail to friends or family might seem convenient, but it also exposes sensitive financial information to unnecessary risk. These documents often contain personal details that could increase your chances of identity theft or fraud if they end up in the wrong hands.
- **Smooth future transactions:** Loan applications, investment accounts, and even simple wire transfers can get delayed or denied if your bank records don't line up with your real residency.

Pro Tip

- Large US retail banks are notorious for taking drastic action if they discover you live abroad, and with today's compliance tools, it's easier than ever for them to find out. In certain cases, they may liquidate your assets and mail you a check. That might sound harmless, but it can trigger large capital gains or unexpected tax consequences you never anticipated. Updating your information proactively helps you stay in control rather than letting your bank make decisions for you.

GLOBAL DIVERSIFICATION FOR GLOBAL LIFESTYLES

As an expat, your financial life is now global, and that means you need to think beyond the dollar.

- **Currency risk:** Even if your brokerage account is with a US custodian and all your statements are in dollars, the real story is in the underlying assets. Take the Vanguard FTSE Europe ETF (VGK) as an example. You buy and sell shares in US dollars, but the companies inside the fund earn revenue in euros, pounds, and Swiss francs. That exposure creates both international diversification and currency diversification. A weaker dollar could boost the value of your foreign holdings when converted back, while a stronger dollar could reduce it.

  Currency diversification is not about speculating on exchange rates or timing short-term currency swings. It's about protecting your long-term purchasing power in the currencies where you'll eventually spend your money. If the dollar weakens, having assets tied to other currencies cushions you. If the dollar strengthens, you're still covered because your core accounts remain dollar based.
- **Foreign exposure:** International stocks and bonds also help smooth out portfolio risk. Yes, there are years when US stocks dominate, but there are also stretches when international markets lead. By holding both, you're less reliant on a single country's economic fortunes.
- **Lifestyle match:** If your retirement spending will eventually be in euros, Swiss francs, or yen, having part of your portfolio tied to those currencies can act as a hedge. You don't need to perfectly match every future expense, but holding a blend of global assets reduces the risk that currency swings derail your long-term plans.

Pro Tip

- Near-term goals (i.e., those less than three years in the future), like saving for a home purchase, tuition, or a major trip, should always be held in the currency you'll spend them in. That way, you don't risk losing purchasing power if exchange rates move against you just before you need the money.

Expert Insight: *What if you're not planning to return to the United States?*

If you've built your life in Singapore, or plan to retire in Australia, concentrating everything in US dollars may not align with your long-term goals. While the United States has some of the largest and most liquid markets in the world, it shouldn't be the only lens through which expats view their investments.

A more thoughtful approach considers where you will ultimately spend your money. Investing in assets denominated in the currencies tied to your future lifestyle can help align your portfolio with your real-world needs.

In some cases, direct investments in individual stocks and bonds can also help avoid PFIC complications, while certain custodians can still provide consolidated US tax reporting through forms like the 1099.

For most expats, the goal isn't to choose between the United States and the rest of the world; it's to build a portfolio that reflects a truly global life.

— Ann Marie Regal, CFP, CEO, Avrio Wealth

AVOIDING INVESTMENT LANDMINES ABROAD

Investments that work great for locals may not be so great for expats. At some point, you may be tempted to invest locally, like when your new bank offers access to a "balanced fund" or your colleague suggests putting money in a tax-advantaged account. In all cases, even those where the recommendation is considered standard best practice to all locals and even other non-US foreigners, proceed with caution.

- **Passive Foreign Investment Companies (PFICs):** A big landmine for US expats is the PFIC rule. Many foreign (non-US) mutual funds, ETFs, and other pooled investment vehicles are classified as PFICs by the IRS. And here's the kicker: what looks like a normal, tax-friendly investment or retirement account in your new country can turn into a nightmare on your US tax return.

Why you need to pay attention and ask questions:

- **Punishing taxation:** PFICs are subject to the highest marginal tax rate on gains and often come with interest charges on top. In many cases, you'll pay far more tax than you would have if you'd invested in a US-based fund.
- **Complex reporting:** Owning even a single PFIC triggers the dreaded **Form 8621**. Each fund requires its own form, and the reporting is notoriously complex and time-consuming (read: tax preparers charge extra for it).
- **Hidden traps:** Local "tax-advantaged" accounts (like Canadian TFSAs, UK ISAs, German Private Rentenversicherungs, and French Assurance Vies) often hold PFICs. While these accounts may be tax-free or tax-advantageous locally, the IRS doesn't recognize them as such.
- **Local products:** Just because something is common in your new country doesn't mean it's US-friendly. That "balanced fund" your bank offers or the tax-free account your neighbor swears by may come with painful consequences once the IRS gets involved.

    Always ask the question: "How will this be taxed in the United States?" before putting money into any local investment. Many foreign products, mutual funds, ETFs, and insurance-linked savings plans are often considered PFICs or trigger other complex reporting.

Even if the product promises tax advantages locally, the cost of IRS reporting (through forms like 8621 or 3520) and the punitive tax treatment can erase any benefit. That's why it's smart to have a US tax accountant who specializes in international issues review these products before you commit. Spending a little on professional advice upfront could save you thousands in unnecessary taxes and reporting fees later.

Expert Insight: *Investing as a US expat can become more complex than many people expect. Many Americans build portfolios using US mutual funds or exchange-traded funds (ETFs), assuming they can continue investing the same way after moving abroad. In reality, while most custodians allow you to keep and sell existing mutual fund holdings, purchasing additional shares is often restricted once you reside outside the United States due to distribution regulations.*

ETFs can offer more flexibility, but even then, foreign regulations, particularly in the European Union, may limit your ability to buy US-domiciled funds unless your account is managed by a professional advisor.

Beyond access, taxation is where things become even more nuanced. The way your investments and retirement accounts are taxed can change significantly based on where you establish residency. While US tax rules continue to apply, your country of residence will also impose its own system, and the two don't always align.

Tax treaties rarely eliminate complexity. Capital gains, for example, may be calculated differently or taxed at different rates abroad. Some countries offer preferential treatment for individual stocks but not for US-listed ETFs, creating unexpected outcomes for investors who assume consistency across borders.

Employer-sponsored retirement accounts such as 401(k)s and 403(b)s are generally less affected by these restrictions and can typically be maintained without major disruption. However, that doesn't mean they should be ignored.

(Continued)

(Continued)

> *The key takeaway: what worked before your move may not work the same way after. Understanding both systems in advance allows you to structure your investments more intentionally and avoid costly surprises.*
>
> *—Otto Rivera, CFP®, EA, Mindful Wealth*

Red Flag Products Abroad (Proceed with Caution)

These accounts or investments (some mentioned earlier) may be tax-advantaged locally but are often **unfriendly for US taxpayers:**

- **UK Individual Savings Accounts (ISAs)**—tax-free in the United Kingdom, but fully taxable in the United States
- **Canadian Tax-Free Savings Accounts (TFSAs)**—same problem as ISAs; no recognition from the IRS.
- **Swiss Pillar 3 retirement accounts**—treated like a taxable brokerage account in the United States and often filled with PFICs that are taxed punitively
- **Foreign mutual funds and ETFs**—usually treated as PFICs with punitive IRS tax rates
- **Foreign life insurance savings policies**—often considered investment contracts subject to complex reporting

> **Pro Tip**
>
> - Even if your local banker is highly recommending something for you, check with a country-specific US expat tax advisor to confirm how the IRS views the account type and investments before investing anything.

THE FLIP SIDE: WHEN LOCAL COUNTRIES DON'T RECOGNIZE US ACCOUNTS

Just as the IRS often fails to recognize foreign tax shelters, your new country may not fully recognize US tax-incentivized accounts. This creates the opposite problem:

- **Roth IRAs**—tax-free in the United States, but distributions are typically treated as taxable by foreign countries; may be treated as taxable in your resident country.
- **Traditional IRAs, Rollover IRAs, and 401(k)s**—tax-deferred in the United States, but some countries may tax growth inside the account as it accrues or fail to recognize the deferral altogether. That makes pre-planning around account type and investment selection a critical part of your move.
- **Health Savings Accounts (HSAs)**—highly tax-advantaged in the United States, but often viewed as taxable brokerage accounts abroad.
- **Education Savings Accounts (ESAs) and 529 Plans**—tax-free growth and withdrawals in the United States, but many countries tax them along the way or deny treaty protection.
- **US ETFs and mutual funds**—while efficient and tax-friendly in the United States, may face penalties or higher taxes in some countries if they're not locally domiciled or registered for sale. Under **MiFID II** (an EU regulation), US fund providers generally cannot distribute to EU residents because they don't provide the required key information documents (KIDs). This can block access to US funds entirely for investors living in the European Union, even if your US brokerage account remains open.

Even in countries that have tax treaties with the United States, recognition of these accounts is inconsistent at best.

Why this matters: You can no longer have a purely US-centric view of your finances. Instead, you need to balance how the US treats your accounts with how your resident country treats them. The "square peg in a round hole" problem is real, and it doesn't always line up neatly.

Workaround: The solution is not one-size-fits-all. The most reliable approach is to work with a qualified custodian or investment management firm that specifically supports US expats. These firms understand cross-border restrictions and can guide you to products you can actually access, without putting you at risk of regulatory or reporting issues.

That's why working with a cross-border professional or a local tax accountant familiar with US account types is essential. They can help you spot mismatches early and avoid being double taxed on accounts you assumed were "safe."

Pro Tip

- If your current financial advisor, tax preparer, or legal team doesn't have experience with cross-border issues, don't assume they can continue to support you effectively once you decided to move abroad. International taxation and investment rules are highly specialized. Look for an advisor with proven expertise in expat matters, ideally someone familiar with the rules in your target country to ensure your team isn't "learning on the job" (with your money) and missing valuable planning opportunities.

BUILDING A CROSS-BORDER PORTFOLIO

Think of your portfolio as your passport; it needs to work across borders. That often means building on a few key principles:

- Anchor in simplicity: Keep your core holdings in US-based ETFs or index funds. They're typically low-cost, tax-efficient, and easy to manage from abroad.
- Know your alternatives: If US ETFs are restricted in your jurisdiction or taxed punitively in your new country, consider a direct indexing approach or locally compliant funds that still give you broad market exposure.
- Add international exposure with intention: Use US-domiciled global funds for clean tax treatment or explore local accounts if a tax treaty protects them. Don't assume what's popular locally is US-friendly.
- Understand reporting differences: US tax reporting is often more detailed than local reporting, but that's a guideline, not a rule. Keeping a US custodian can help lower costs, since they issue clear US tax forms like 1099s or 1099-Rs. Be aware, however, that these don't always translate abroad.
- Stay flexible: Your portfolio should evolve as your life abroad changes. The strategy that works in year one in Dubai may need to be adjusted by year five in Germany.

Common Reporting Mismatches for Expats

- **Dividends:** The US splits dividends into *qualified* and *ordinary*. Many countries don't. Local preparers sometimes add both numbers together, overstating your income and causing double reporting.
- **Capital gains:** The US calculates gains in US dollars. Many countries require local currency calculations at the purchase and sale dates. You could have a gain in one system and a loss in the other.
- **Retirement accounts:** Traditional IRAs, Roth IRAs, 401(k)s, and HSAs are tax-advantaged in the United States but may be treated

as taxable brokerage accounts abroad—creating surprises if not planned for.

- **Reporting forms:** A US custodian's 1099 or 1099-R works perfectly for the IRS, but those forms don't always satisfy local requirements. Expect two sets of tax paperwork each year.

> **Pro Tip**
> - Before filing locally, review how income, gains, and retirement accounts are being reported. Small misclassifications can create big, avoidable tax bills.

QUICK CHECKLIST

- **Confirm your US brokerage accounts can stay open abroad**. Call your custodian before moving; policies vary widely.
- **Open and fund accounts before leaving the United States**. This is especially important for state-specific accounts such as 529 college savings plans or custodial accounts (UGMA/UTMA). Once abroad, opening new ones may not be possible, even with an expat-friendly custodian or planner. But remember, opening the account is only half the job. You also need to understand how it will be taxed in your new country. For example, a 529 plan is tax-free in the United States but may be fully taxable abroad.
- **Know the product restrictions**. Your investment menu may change once you move. You may lose the ability to purchase certain **US mutual funds** or **ETFs** (though you can usually continue holding them). Restrictions come from both:
  - **US custodians** may limit what expats can trade or which accounts they can maintain.

    - **Local regulations**, such as **MiFID II** in the EU, might block access to many US funds because providers don't issue the required KIDs.
- **Keep key US accounts open at first**. Don't rush to close checking, credit card, or brokerage accounts until you know you're settled abroad.
- **Update your address with US financial institutions when appropriate**. You don't need to do it on day one, but once you've built a life abroad (permanent housing, job, residence permit), you should. Failing to do so risks account freezes or forced liquidations, which can create surprise taxable gains.
- **Review your portfolio's currency exposure**. Think about where you'll spend in the future (euros, francs, yen) and align part of your portfolio accordingly.
- **Plan for flexibility**. The strategy that works in Dubai in year one may not fit Germany by year five. Each relocation can bring new tax rules, investment restrictions, and currency considerations, meaning your financial plan and portfolio may need a full update. Build with adaptability in mind so your portfolio can evolve alongside your expat journey.

CHAPTER EIGHT

HOW DO I ACTUALLY BUILD AN INVESTMENT PORTFOLIO AS A US EXPAT?

Key Question: "What does a practical, tax-aware investment portfolio actually look like for a US expat?"

By now, you've handled the defensive moves: you've secured your US accounts, reduced the odds of account freezes, and learned what not to do. Now we shift into the productive work: building a portfolio that supports the life you're building abroad.

The fundamentals of investing don't change when you move overseas. The rules of risk, diversification, and compounding still apply.

What changes is the implementation: what you can buy, where you can hold it, how it's taxed, and who is allowed to advise you.

This chapter gives you a practical way forward. You'll see examples of simple exchange-traded fund (ETF) portfolios, alternatives when US ETFs aren't available, and ways to adapt when local regulations or taxes create constraints.

HOW TO USE THIS CHAPTER

You don't need to read this chapter straight through.

- If you're new to investing, start with Part I to build your foundation: risk, time horizon, and simple portfolio structure.
- If you already invest and want to do it safely as an expat, start with Part II, where we build simple ETF portfolios that work for many Americans abroad.
- If you live in the European Union or United Kingdom, go to Part III. This is where investing gets more technical because US ETFs may be restricted for retail investors.
- If DIY isn't your thing, or your situation is complex, skim Part IV early so you understand what professional support can realistically look like in the expat world.

Location, Location, Location

It's not just a tag line for real estate agents; it's also a critical piece of the puzzle for the globally mobile investor.

Where in the world are you?

- **The "pre-mover":** You're still in the United States, you probably already have some form of investment account, a 401(k), an IRA, or even a taxable brokerage account. You want to understand the financial implications of where you will go next. That "where" falls into two main categories (with many different subcategories!).

- **The whole world (minus the European Union):** You are not in the United States, but you're also not in the European Union, you're in the rest of the world, and it's a wide, wide world. You have options, but the rules aren't the same for you as they are for your still-in-the-US counterparts, so you need to be aware of the traps, and there are many!
- **The EU/UK resident:** You're living the dream, and simultaneously stuck between a rock (US tax rules) and a hard place (EU investment regulations). You are in (or soon moving to) a highly regulated zone. Your goal: Avoid the "MiFID II/PFIC" trap and understand why your DIY options just got a lot smaller. Part III is where we break down the investing options you have.

Regardless of which category you fall into, Part I (Foundations) is your universal starting point. Part II explains how to invest using a simple two fund portfolio that will support investors in most of the world, and Part III breaks down the more complex workarounds available for Americans in the European Union and United Kingdom.

PART I: THE FOUNDATIONS OF EXPAT INVESTING

When it comes to investing, there's one principle that holds true whether you're in Boston, Berlin, or Bangkok: costs matter. Decades of research (and common sense) show that keeping fees low and spreading your bets widely across the market is one of the surest paths to long-term success. That's why many investors, expats included, start with a low-cost, broadly diversified portfolio.

Start with Understanding Risk

Before we talk about *what* to invest in, we need to talk about *you*.

Personal finance is personal. When it comes to finance, math skills, a good calculator, and a spreadsheet should solve the issue. Unfortunately, personal finance involves more than just numbers; it's the intersection of you, your history, emotional state, values, goals, and experiences, all tangled up *with* the math. As a result of all the elements that go into managing your personal finances, it's quite common to experience fear and uncertainty when you arrive to the topic.

How to Manage Your Fear

The biggest fear most investors begin with is the fear of losing their hard-earned savings. Most people are aware that trying to time the market is ill-advised at best, but it's also common for novices to fear the fluctuations associated with investing. "What if I lose everything?" you might wonder.

Losing all your money simply isn't a realistic outcome if you are invested wisely, which we will discuss later. That said, I do want to validate that fear is a normal feeling when risk is in the picture, and there's always an element of risk when it comes to investing. However, there are ways to manage risk, both as it appears in your portfolio and how it manifests in your mind. Managing risk means being able to stay invested when markets are volatile (read: going up and down or even taking a nosedive) and headlines are loud and driving panic. Keep in mind: volatility is not a flaw of investing; it's actually a perfectly standard feature of long-term growth.

Evaluating Your Risk Tolerance

Understanding your unique ability to tolerate risk and your overall need to accept risk is the foundation of how you decide what to invest in. For most investors, you're going to want most of your assets in stocks (high volatility and high growth potential), some of your assets in bonds (moderate volatility and moderate growth), and only a small amount of your assets in cash as your emergency fund (no volatility, but negative real growth due to inflation).

The percentage of your assets held in stocks versus bonds is referred to as your asset allocation, and in order to choose an asset allocation, you need to understand yourself and your unique situation first.

For expats, this matters even more. Living abroad can add emotional and logistical layers to investing: currency fluctuations, political uncertainty, changing residency plans, and being far from familiar systems. These factors can make market swings feel more intense, even when your underlying strategy remains sound.

Risk Is Emotional and Mathematical

Many investors believe managing risk is purely rational. They understand markets rise and fall, so they assume they're comfortable with risk. In practice, managing risk is just as emotional as it is mathematical.

A well-designed portfolio is not the one with the highest theoretical return; it's the one you can stick with during uncomfortable periods. If your portfolio causes anxiety or leads you to abandon your plan during downturns, it's too aggressive, regardless of what the numbers say. Likewise, if your portfolio is too conservative in terms of volatility, you may fall short or never achieve your long-term financial goals, such as being able to rely on passive income from your investments in your retirement. It's a balancing act between volatility on one hand and inflation, opportunity cost, and longevity risk on the other.

> **Expert Insight:** *Fortunes are made by being highly concentrated, but fortunes are preserved by being highly diversified.*
>
> *—Brian Wruk, MBA, CFP®(US), CFP®(Canada), TEP, CIM, RFP®,*
> *Transitional Financial Advisors*

Risk Tolerance, Risk Capacity, and Risk Need

These three concepts are related but distinct:

- **Risk tolerance:** How much volatility you can emotionally handle.
- **Risk capacity:** How much risk your financial situation allows you to take, based on income stability, emergency savings, and time horizon.
- **Risk need:** The level of return required to meet your goals.

A successful investment strategy sits at the intersection of all three. You may need growth to reach long-term goals, but your portfolio still needs to align with your comfort level and real-life constraints, especially when navigating life abroad.

While no 10-question quiz can capture your entire emotional history with money, you need a baseline. You need to move from "feeling" to "data."

A Helpful Starting Point: Vanguard's Investor Questionnaire

I am a big fan of Vanguard's investment philosophy: low costs, broad diversification, and long-term discipline. While Vanguard is not accessible to US expats as a custodian, their Investor Questionnaire is one of the clearest (and free!) tools available to help individuals assess their risk tolerance.

You can find it here:

🔗https://investor.vanguard.com/tools-calculators/investor-questionnaire

The questionnaire focuses on your reactions to market declines, your time horizon, and your comfort with short-term losses in pursuit of long-term gains. Your results are not a prescription; they are a starting point to help clarify whether a conservative, balanced, or growth-oriented asset allocation is best for you

Bottom line: If you can't sleep when the market drops, the math doesn't matter—you're too aggressive.

Translating Risk into a Portfolio

Once you understand your risk profile, the next step is turning that insight into an actual investment portfolio. This is where structure matters, not complexity.

One investing principle holds true no matter where you live: costs matter. Decades of research show that keeping fees low and diversifying broadly across markets is one of the most reliable ways to build long-term wealth. For most investors, including expats, this means starting with a simple, diversified portfolio built with low-cost index funds or ETFs.

At its most basic level, a diversified portfolio includes exposure to

- **US stocks**, for long-term growth,
- **international stocks**, for global diversification, and
- **bonds or other fixed income**, for stability and income.

For many people, this is enough. A portfolio like this is easy to manage, keeps costs low, and avoids the risk of betting your future on a single company, sector, or country.

Time Horizon

It's important to understand the timeline for your investments. While equity (stocks) are a very good long-term investment, they're terrible over short time horizons due to all of that volatility we just spoke about. This is why the money that you invest should be invested for the long term, meaning the rest of your life. Even if you're five years from retirement, you're still investing for 20+ years based on average life expectancy.

The goal here isn't to build up a rainy-day fund, but to create a passive income from your investments. To do that, you need to keep most of your money invested and live off the growth. The 4% rule is a useful planning tool. This is a well-researched rule of thumb that shows that if you take out 4% of the initial value of your portfolio every year (adjusted for inflation), your portfolio will last for 30 years or more. So effectively, you're keeping 96% (or more!) of your money invested even after you start living off the funds.

So what about all those short-term goals? That's what savings accounts are for.

Asset Allocation: Stocks vs. Bonds

The mix between stocks and bonds is the primary driver of both risk and return in your portfolio.

- **More stocks** generally mean higher growth potential, but with greater short-term volatility.
- **More bonds** tend to reduce volatility and provide smoother returns, but with lower long-term growth.

Your allocation should reflect your risk tolerance, time horizon, and lifestyle needs. As you move closer to your funding goals, retirement is often your largest funding goal, portfolios typically shift gradually from stocks toward bonds. This helps protect the wealth you've built and reduces the risk of a market downturn right when you begin drawing on your savings.

There is no universally "correct" allocation. A 60/40 portfolio may feel right for one investor, while another with a longer runway and higher risk tolerance may be 90/10. It is important to note that you need at minimum 50% of your portfolio in equity in order to create a passive income from your portfolio that will last for 30 or more years. The goal here is alignment with your unique situation, not optimization on a spreadsheet.

PART II: ETF-BASED PORTFOLIOS: BOGLEHEADS STYLE

I'm a fan of the Bogleheads approach, named after Jack Bogle, the founder of Vanguard, which is built on the following core principles:

- Develop a workable plan.
- Invest early and often.
- Never bear too much or too little risk.
- Diversify.
- Never try to time the market.
- Use index funds when possible.
- Keep costs low.
- Minimize taxes.
- Invest with simplicity.
- Diversify broadly.

This framework works extremely well for expats, with one important caveat: you must account for cross-border rules, taxes, and product availability.

I often reference Vanguard funds because they are widely known, high-quality, and low-cost, but they are not the only option. Comparable US ETFs are available from providers such as Schwab, Fidelity, iShares, and others. While Vanguard itself is not typically expat-friendly as a custodian, Vanguard ETFs can often be accessed through platforms that do support US expats, such as Charles Schwab or Interactive Brokers.

Investing terms

- **Ticker:** the code or symbol for a stock or ETF, typically a combination of a few letters and/or numbers.

- **Expense ratio:** the total cost you pay the provider of a fund, expressed as a percentage. Most index funds have a total expense ratio of less than 1%. Some are as low as 0.05%
- **Rebalancing:** As prices fluctuate, the balance between your stock and bond holdings will change; rebalancing is simply resetting the balance of your portfolio back to your chosen asset allocation by buying the lagging fund with new savings or selling some of the overperforming fund and reallocating it to the other lagging asset class.

A Sample Allocation: 80/20

As an illustration, consider a portfolio with

- **80% stocks** and
- **20% bonds.**

This is often described as a "growth with a cushion" portfolio. It offers meaningful long-term growth potential while still providing some downside protection during market declines.

This example is not a recommendation. Your personal allocation should be based on your risk tolerance, time horizon, and financial situation. Think of these portfolios as starting points, not prescriptions. Table 8.1 illustrates how three dimensions translate into four common starting-point allocations.

Keep in mind, even for the same investor, there are times when your risk tolerance, capacity, and need will change. If you're investing a large lump sum as a first-time investor, you may have a lower risk tolerance than someone who has been slowly and steadily investing from their monthly savings for years. It's okay to start off more conservative and

Table 8.1 Three dimensions translated into four common starting-point allocations.

Sample 80/20 allocation

Growth with a cushion

- 80% stocks—long-term growth engine
- 20% bonds—downside buffer

This is an illustration, not a recommendation. Your allocation should reflect your own risk tolerance, timeline, and goals.

Allocation comparison by risk profile

Allocation	Risk tolerance	Risk capacity (timeline)	Risk need (growth)
60 / 40	Nervous or cautious about market swings	Very short or inflexible timeline	Low—goals reachable without much growth
70 / 30	Cautious about volatility	Moderate flexibility on timeline	Some growth needed to reach financial independence
80 / 20	Tolerant of volatility	Flexible timeline to FI	Moderate growth needed to reach FI target
90 / 10	Unbothered by short-term swings	Very flexible or very long timeline	Substantial growth required to hit FI target

RISK TOLERANCE	RISK CAPACITY	RISK NEED
How you feel about market swings	**How long before you need the money**	**How much growth your goals require**

ratchet up as you build a stronger risk tolerance muscle over time. It's also much easier to stomach a 40% loss if it's only "paper gains" and not your actual hard-earned savings that's disappearing on the screen. (Remember, it's only a loss if you sell, until then it's just theoretical.) Think of your portfolio like a house. If the market value of your home drops $50k today, you haven't lost money unless you sell the house and move out. Investing is the same.

EXAMPLE PORTFOLIOS FOR US EXPATS WHO CAN (AND *SHOULD*) ACCESS US ETFs

Starting Out as a DIY Expat Investor

At this stage, your goal is to start investing and keep it simple. You don't need 10 funds; you need a solid foundation. Here is an example two-fund portfolio:

- **80% Global Equity ETF** (e.g., VT—Vanguard Total World Stock)
- **20% Bond ETF** (e.g., BNDW—Vanguard Total World Bond Market)

It may be boring, but it's globally diversified, cheap to run, and easy to rebalance.

This portfolio is diversified, low cost, and easy to manage. For many people, this will be where they stay for most of their time investing, with modifications to the asset allocation as you learn more about your own risk tolerance or your risk capacity or need for risk changes over time.

The key is that any changes to your investing plan are made based on changes in your life, not based on changes in the market news or performance. The idea here is that you have an all-weather plan that will get you through to financial independence. Being reactionary will accomplish the opposite of that.

> **Expert Insight:** *Many expats worry about buying US dollar ETFs. Remember: Global diversification (owning non-US companies) is itself*

> *a currency hedge, even if the ETF is traded in dollars. The currency an equity ETF is traded in is irrelevant; it's the underlying assets that determine the fund's value. While we want our equity to be global, we want our bonds to match the currency we plan to spend in the future if possible because bonds do carry currency risk.*
>
> *—Blair Hoover, CYO Finance*

The longer you're invested, the more experience you will have navigating the volatility of the market. Your first $100,000 invested is a big milestone, it's worth celebrating, and it's also a great time to reevaluate your asset allocation. You may decide to increase your equity allocation if you've proven to yourself you won't flinch in a market crash, or you may find that you value stability more than you thought. Some will want a more aggressive allocation, some a less aggressive one. It's highly personal, but by this point you've got "skin in the game," and you should have a bit more confidence in what you're doing.

There is no reason to complicate your portfolio; in fact, the more funds you're managing, the more likely it is that you make a behavioral mistake. We're looking for time in the market, not timing the market. For most people, you will reap higher returns by keeping your portfolio painfully simple.

No matter how much you have invested, once you have invested assets, you're going to benefit from tax planning. As an American, it's likely that you will need a US cross border tax planner *and* possibly a local cross-border tax planner. It is crucial to speak with a knowledgeable tax planner before you move countries. Often, optimizations can be made that more than compensate for the fees you pay your tax advisor.

Your First $500,000 as a DIY Expat Investor

Hitting $500,000 is a real milestone. You're no longer "getting started." Your portfolio is now a meaningful part of your long-term security, and small decisions, fees, taxes, portfolio structure, start to matter more.

This is a great point to pause and ask a different set of questions than you asked at $50,000:

- Where do I realistically expect to live for the next 5–10 years?
- What currency am I most likely to spend in long term?
- Do I want to keep this portfolio globally generic, or start tailoring it to where my life is actually rooted?

If you're settled in one country (or fairly confident you'll stay in one region or currency), you may have opportunities to align your portfolio more closely with

- your long-term spending currency,
- local tax treatment of certain investments,
- estate or inheritance considerations, and
- local rules around bonds, funds, or reporting.

That can be valuable. But it comes with a cost.

Customization Adds Complexity

Adding regional tilts, local bond exposure, or country-specific tax moves can improve efficiency, but it also increases complexity. And complexity is a real risk for DIY investors.

For many DIY investors, the best "next level" portfolio at $500,000 is not a complicated one. It's a clean, well-structured two- to four-fund portfolio that you can maintain through busy seasons, market volatility, and future moves. Ask yourself, "Can I manage this consistently without second-guessing myself or creating tax/reporting problems?"

This is also the point where professional support becomes more accessible.

Many firms that work with US expats set minimums around this level. And the economics start to make more sense:

- **AUM management** is often around **1% of assets** (so ~$5,000/year on a $500,000 portfolio).
- **Flat-fee planning** often lands in the **$5,000–$15,000/year** range depending on complexity.

Those fees can be worth it if you want a hands-off or collaborative approach, if you're navigating multiple tax systems, or if you're ready to integrate investments with deeper tax and estate planning. At this stage, avoiding one major mistake, or capturing one missed planning opportunity, can easily cover the cost.

For the Committed DIY Investor

Plenty of investors manage seven-figure portfolios on their own using a simple structure like the two-fund portfolio in this chapter. DIY can absolutely scale.

The difference at $500,000 is that your margin for error shrinks. The stakes are higher, and tax drag or behavioral mistakes become more expensive. So, the goal isn't to "graduate" into complexity. The goal is to choose the level of simplicity you can sustain and get help where it improves your outcome.

Important Reminder

- The example portfolios in this chapter assume you can access US-domiciled ETFs from abroad. Not every US expat can.

In some jurisdictions, most notably the European Union under MiFID II rules, US ETFs are restricted because they do not provide the required key information documents (KIDs). If you live in the European Union or United Kingdom, your ability to buy these products may be limited or blocked entirely (see Part III for practical workarounds).

Even where access is technically allowed, foreign tax treatment can still derail the strategy. Some countries classify US ETFs as foreign funds and tax them more harshly than local equivalents. In those cases, what looks like a low-cost, tax-efficient investment from a US perspective can turn into a high-tax outcome abroad.

This is where cross-border advice adds real value. Product access and tax treatment don't always line up intuitively, and many expats only discover the mismatch after the damage is done. It's a classic case of *you don't know what you don't know*, and one of the most common reasons otherwise solid investment plans fall apart internationally.

Always check two things before investing:

1. **Custodian rules:** Will your US brokerage allow you to trade this product from your country of residence?
2. **Local tax rules:** How will your new country classify and tax the investment?

But don't forget taxes: Even on a temporary assignment, you may trigger local tax filing obligations. Many countries tax residents (and sometimes even certain nonresidents) on a global basis, not just local earnings. That means:

- You may owe local tax filings even if all your accounts remain in the United States.
- Reporting obligations often extend to your worldwide portfolio, even if you never move a dollar locally.

Translation: You need to balance investment access (what products you can buy under US + local rules) with tax compliance (what your host country expects you to report).

READER EXERCISE: CHOOSING THE RIGHT INVESTMENT FRAMEWORK AS AN EXPAT

Use this checklist to help you determine **which approach fits your current situation**, and what your next best step should be. There is no "right" answer for everyone. The goal is alignment, not perfection.

Step 1: Confirm Your Risk Profile

- ☐ I have a clear sense of my risk tolerance (how I emotionally handle market ups and downs).
- ☐ I understand my time horizon for the money I'm investing.
- ☐ I know whether I prioritize growth, stability, or a balance of both.

Use this information to choose an asset allocation that helps you sleep at night but will also allow your passive income to last as long as you live (not less than 50% equity). See Figure 8.1.

Step 2: Check Your Investment Access

- ☐ My US brokerage allows me to buy and hold US-domiciled ETFs from my country of residence.

Figure 8.1 Common risk profiles.

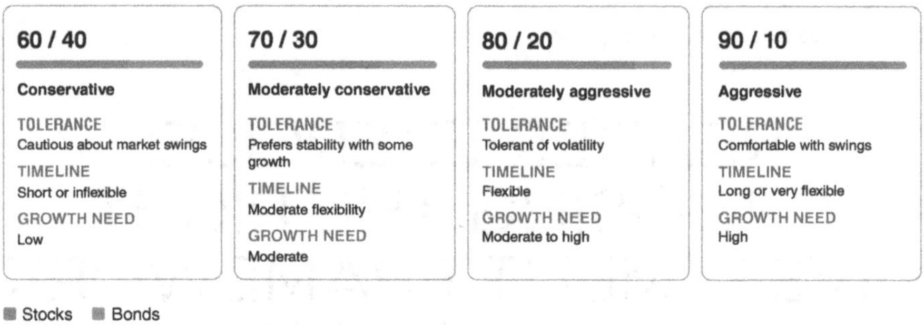

- ☐ I understand whether local regulations (e.g., MiFID II in the EU) restrict ETF access.
- ☐ I know whether my current residence taxes US ETFs unfavorably.

If you are unable to access US-domiciled ETFs skip to part III to read about workarounds. If your country of residence taxes US ETFs unfavorably, seek out a cross-border tax planner from your country of residence that works with Americans.

Step 3: Assess Your Portfolio Size

Check the box that best reflects where your investment portfolio is *today* (not where you plan to be):

- ☐ Under $100,000—Focus on simplicity and getting started
- ☐ $100,000–$500,000—Tax and estate planning awareness starts to matter more, tax planning becomes more important
- ☐ $500,000+—Advanced tax management and professional investing support may be beneficial

Your strategy should evolve as your portfolio grows.

Step 4: Evaluate Tax Complexity

- ☐ I understand how to file my US and country of residence (if applicable) taxes annually.
- ☐ I understand how capital gains will be taxed by the United States.
- ☐ I am aware of how my country of residence taxes investments and capital gains.
- ☐ I have a plan to reduce my current and future tax exposure in both the United States and my country of residence (if applicable).

The more assets you have, the more you have to gain from professional tax planning—not just tax filing. If you were not able to check most of the previous boxes, you will probably benefit from working with a cross-border tax professional.

Step 5: Consider Concentration Risk

- ☐ A large portion of my income or equity compensation is tied to one sector (e.g., tech).
- ☐ I live or plan to spend the long-term in a country other than the United States.
- ☐ Most of my assets are concentrated in a country where I no longer reside (e.g., property, stocks, bonds, cash savings).

If you checked any of these boxes, you may need to look at diversifying your existing assets in addition to building a diversified portfolio while living abroad.

Step 6: Choose Your Current Framework

Based on your previous answers, which approach best fits you **right now**?

- ☐ **DIY ETF-based Portfolio**
  Best if you have access to US ETFs and want a simple approach you can manage yourself. This is how beginners start building their assets. (If you don't have access to US-based ETFs skip to part III.)
- ☐ **Hybrid or Advisor-supported Approach**
  Best if your portfolio is growing, your tax situation is complex, or you want professional oversight.
- ☐ **Fee-only Asset Management**
  Often an option if your portfolio is already $500,000 as advisors need to show you are a qualified investor. You must be cautious of nonfiduciary advisors in the expat space and also cautious of US advisors who don't understand the financial implications of the country where you reside. An advisor who "only" manages your US portfolio without understanding the tax and financial implications in your resident country isn't doing you any favors.

Remember: This choice is not permanent. Many expats move between these frameworks as their lives and assets evolve starting with a more DIY approach and engaging professionals as their wealth and complexity increases.

PART III: THE "HARD MODE" WORKAROUND (EU AND RESTRICTED ZONES)

For the investor in the European Union or United Kingdom, the "Standard Path" of buying US ETFs often hits a wall. Due to MiFID II regulations, US ETFs cannot provide the specific paperwork (KIDs) required to be sold to retail investors in Europe. US regulations prevent what EU regulations require. It's complicated.

If you find yourself in this "hard mode" zone, you essentially have a menu of five options, and as you'll see, none of them is easy.

MiFID Workaround

Under MiFID II, US citizens with EU residency generally can't buy US ETFs directly on their own. However, they *can* access them when working with a professional investment advisor who has the right permissions. That said:

- Not all advisors or firms will work with US expats due to compliance hurdles.
- Many firms that specialize in expats set minimum investment requirements (often $500k+), which can make this path harder for new investors.

Temporary Assignments in Europe

If you're in Europe on a short-term or exploratory assignment, it can make sense to delay updating your brokerage address until you've confirmed the move is permanent. Once a custodian treats you as an EU resident, MiFID II restrictions may limit your ability to buy US ETFs. Keeping a US address a bit longer, while staying compliant with tax rules, can preserve flexibility while you decide whether Europe is a stop or a long-term home.

1. **EU-domiciled ETFs (The PFIC Trap)**
    - **The Allure:** "If I can't buy US ETFs, I'll just buy the European versions (UCITS)."
    - **The Reality: Hard No.** For US citizens, these are classified as Passive Foreign Investment Companies (PFICs). The US tax treatment is

punitive, involving complex paperwork and potential tax rates that can eat up more than your gains. Unless you have a multi-million dollar portfolio and a very specialized team, avoid this.

2. **Elective Professional Status**
   - **The Allure:** Opt out of MiFID II regulations by being categorized as a "Professional Investor."
   - **The Reality:** Difficult to qualify. Most brokers (like IBKR) require you to meet at least two of three criteria: a €500k+ portfolio, significant professional experience in finance, or a high volume of large trades. It's a narrow gate that is closed to most.
3. **Using Options to "Backdoor" into ETFs**
   - **The Allure:** You can't *buy* the ETF, but you can exercise an option to acquire the shares.
   - **The Reality:** It requires a level of technical trading skill that most DIY investors aren't equipped to manage.
4. **DIY Direct Investing**
   - **The Allure:** Buy the individual stocks that make up an index (like the S&P 500) one by one.
   - **The Reality:** High behavioral risk. While this bypasses the conflicting EU–US rules, it is difficult to set up, exhausting to rebalance, and creates the temptation to "tinker" with your stocks, the exact opposite of the "Stay the Course" philosophy.
5. **Hiring a Professional Manager**
   - **The Allure:** Use a firm with "discretionary" management that can access US products on your behalf.
   - **The Reality:** This option is often out of reach for newer investors. Most firms that specialize in cross-border and expat investing impose minimums of $500,000 or more, reflecting the added regulatory and compliance complexity. For those earlier in their investing journey, this path may not be accessible yet—but it can become a viable option as your portfolio grows.

The UK "Reporting Status" Trap

For DIY investors in the United Kingdom, you may hear about US ETFs that have "HMRC Reporting Status." While this status is vital for tax efficiency (it allows gains to be taxed at 20% capital gains rates rather than 45% income tax rates), it does *not* solve your access problem.

Even if a US ETF is "reporting," it still lacks the regulatory KID document required to be sold to UK retail investors. This leaves many DIYers in a double bind: you can't buy the "good" US funds because of UK retail rules, and you shouldn't buy many of the available UK funds because of US PFIC rules. **This is why the "Berkshire Bridge" or professional management often becomes a necessity for Americans in the United Kingdom.**

> **Expert Insights**: *Americans in the UK face a double bind: you can't buy the "good" US funds because of UK retail rules, and you shouldn't buy the available UK funds because of US PFIC rules.*
>
> *—Blair Hoover, CYO Finance*

The Verdict

If you are in the European Union and below the $500,000 threshold, you are in a "regulatory no-man's land." Your focus should be on staying compliant, keeping costs as low as possible within these constraints, and building your assets until you hit the threshold where more doors open up (or the US and EU regulators reconcile their differences).

But what if none of these options work for you? There is one reasonable workaround for those with less capital, less experience, or both. It's not an ideal solution, but it's better than nothing (Table 8.2).

Table 8.2 Investment options for US expats in the EU.

OPTION	THE REALITY CHECK	VERDICT	WHO IT'S USEFUL FOR
EU domiciled ETFs *"I'll just buy the local versions."*	Triggers the PFIC trap — punitive US tax rates and complex Form 8621 filings.	Not recommended	No one
Professional status *"I'll opt out of retail rules."*	Requires meeting two of three: €500k+ portfolio, significant trading activity, or professional finance experience.	High barrier	Those who can qualify
Options backdoor *"I'll use a technical loophole."*	Requires buying in blocks of 100 shares (e.g., $15k+ per trade) and navigating a complex strategy.	High capital	Experienced investors with larger sums to deploy
DIY direct investing *"I'll buy individual stocks."*	Difficult to rebalance and prone to emotional tinkering without a disciplined system.	High maintenance	Investors willing to hire professional support for oversight
Professional manager *"I'll hire a specialist firm."*	Most specialist firms require a $500k minimum investment to take on clients.	Best for larger portfolios	Those with larger portfolios who don't find another workable option

Below the $500,000 threshold, EU-based US expats face a regulatory no-man's land. The priority: stay compliant, keep costs low, and build assets until more doors open.

Tactical Workaround: The "Berkshire Bridge," a Strategy for Regulatory Purgatory

If you find yourself in the "sub-$500k portfolio while residing in the EU trap," there is one "Plan B" worth considering before you dive into direct investing or complex options trading.

Even though you cannot buy a US-domiciled ETF like VT (Vanguard Total World Stock Index), you *can* buy individual stocks while living in the European Union or United Kingdom. Direct indexing is complex, but there is an easy, though not ideal, way to create a somewhat diverse portfolio while only buying a single stock. That's **Berkshire Hathaway.** It's an individual stock that acts somewhat like a diversified portfolio.

You may have heard of Warren Buffett "the Oracle of Omaha." He is a renowned investor who, along with Charlie Munger, started Berkshire Hathaway, a textile manufacturer turned investment holding company. Berkshire Hathaway fully owns or holds shares of companies across many industries. There are two share classes, BRK-A, which trades in the hundreds of thousands of dollars per share, and **BRK-B**, a bit under $500 per share as of 2026. **BRK-B** is the shortcut we're talking about here.

- **Built-in Diversification:** Under one ticker, you own a collection of more than 60 companies (GEICO, BNSF Railway, Duracell) and a massive portfolio of public stocks (like Apple, Coca-Cola, and American Express).
- **No MiFID II Block:** Because it is a single stock, not a "fund," European brokers won't block the trade.
- **Tax Efficiency:** Berkshire does not pay a dividend. For expats in high-tax countries, this is often a blessing; you only pay tax when you sell, allowing your wealth to compound uninterrupted for years.
- **The "Vessel" for Your Cash:** At roughly $500 a share, it's an accessible way to keep your money working in the US economy while you build toward the $500,000 threshold.

The Caveat

- **Concentration risk:** It is still a single company. You are betting on the culture and capital allocation of one firm. It is *not* a replacement for a global two-fund ETF portfolio, but it is often a superior alternative to sitting in 100% cash for a decade while you wait for your portfolio to grow. I wouldn't recommend ONLY buying BRK-B, but it's a starting place and can be complimented with further diversification through direct investing as your portfolio grows.

- **Past results do not predict future success:** Just because BRK-B was a great investment in the past, doesn't mean that it will always remain so. Charlie Munger died in 2023, and Warren Buffet retired at the end of 2025, so the original leaders of the company are no longer calling the shots. This isn't a bad thing; it's an unknown thing.
- **You will still want to diversify further**. If you choose this path, you'll want to add in other companies over time to move toward direct indexing or, if you have access in the future, add in or switch to a broadly diversified index ETF.

If the regulatory hurdles of MiFID II and the tax traps of PFICs feel like a full-time job you didn't sign up for, you aren't alone. For many, this is the point where "DIY" becomes "Do it with help."

PART IV: REALITY CHECKS FOR US EXPAT INVESTORS

Why Professional Help Can Be Hard to Find Early On

If you're below roughly $500,000 in investable assets, it can be surprisingly hard to find an advisor willing to fully manage your investments. That's not because your situation is simple, or because you're "not ready." In fact, it's often the opposite.

Many US expats have *very* complex lives early on: multiple tax systems, uncertain residency plans, restricted investment options, and constant change. Managing that complexity takes time, expertise, and higher compliance costs, which is why many firms set high minimums or focus on wealthier clients.

That doesn't mean you're on your own. If you're just getting started, a strong DIY foundation paired with targeted, hourly advice is often the smartest path. Many cross-border planners and international tax professionals offer one-off projects or short consulting sessions. A single hour with the right expert, before a move, before investing, or before a big decision, can save you years of cleanup and thousands in avoidable mistakes.

You don't need full-service management to get good guidance. You need the *right* guidance, at the *right* moment. As your assets grow, ongoing professional support may start to make sense. Until then, focus on staying compliant, keeping your portfolio simple, and getting help strategically when your life, not just your net worth, gets complicated.

RED FLAGS: COMMON EXPAT INVESTING AND PLANNING MISTAKES

Use this checklist to spot warning signs that your current setup, or the advice you're receiving, may be creating unnecessary risk, cost, or compliance issues.

Advisor and Professional Red Flags

- ☐ **Your US advisor is "happy to keep working with you" but only manages your US assets and has no understanding of how their trades are taxed in your country of residence.**
  If they don't understand how trades are taxed in your country of residence, this is not a favor. A move can turn US-efficient strategies

into foreign tax problems, even when performance looks good on paper.

- ☐ **An advisor tells you to keep using your US address so they can continue to support you.**
  This may be workable during short-term assignments or early transition years. Long term, your address needs to reflect reality. Mismatched residency creates compliance risk and limits future flexibility.
- ☐ **You're relying on "free" advice from an advisor.**
  If you don't clearly understand how someone is paid, you're likely paying more than you would knowingly agree to. Commission-based advisors are often salespeople, not fiduciaries. Their incentive is the product, not your outcome.

  If you hear terms like *"offshore," "savings plan,"* or *"premiums,"* pause immediately. These are often investment-linked insurance products marketed heavily to expats. They typically involve long lock-ins, opaque fee structures (sometimes totaling 6–9%+), and painful exit penalties. They are designed to pay commissions, not to preserve flexibility.
- ☐ **Your local (non-US) advisor doesn't understand US tax rules.**
  Local solutions can be perfectly legal and still disastrous for Americans. PFICs, insurance wrappers, and local funds often create punitive US taxation and complex reporting. A good local strategy is not automatically a good US expat strategy.
- ☐ **Your US accountant has no international experience.**
  Good intentions don't replace expertise. Cross-border mistakes often don't show up immediately—but they are expensive to unwind later.
- ☐ **You're working with a "global generalist" who advises everywhere, equally.**
  High-level guidance can be helpful early on. Once you've chosen a country, depth matters. Tax treaties, investment rules, and planning

opportunities vary dramatically by location. Country-specific specialists bring benefits:

- Deep knowledge of how US rules interact with *that* country
- Awareness of common traps and planning opportunities
- A local professional network (tax, legal, pensions, real estate, schooling)

Successful cross-border planning rarely lives in one silo.

Structural and Planning Red Flags

- ☐ **Your investments don't reflect where you live or plan to spend.** Currency mismatch can quietly add risk to an otherwise solid portfolio.
- ☐ **You own products you can't explain or understand.** Complexity often hides cost, risk, or tax inefficiency. If you don't understand it, someone else is likely benefiting more than you are.
- ☐ **No one is looking at the full picture.** Investments, taxes, residency, and long-term plans are handled in isolation rather than as a coordinated strategy.

If You Recognize One or More of These Red Flags

You're not alone, and you haven't failed. Many expats end up in these situations for various reasons:

- Trusted professionals want to help but lack cross-border expertise.
- The system isn't built for globally mobile lives.
- Good advice in one country doesn't always translate to another.
- Unscrupulous salespeople are more focused on their commissions than your well-being.

How to Use Generalists vs. Specialists

Cross-border generalists are helpful under the following circumstances:

- You're still in the "should we move?" phase.
- You're comparing multiple countries.
- You're looking for support with managing the big picture of your finances.
- You want to grow your understanding of personal finance in general.

Country-specific specialists are essential when the following occurs:

- You've chosen a destination or narrowed it to one country.
- You're structuring investments, compensation, or retirement.
- You're planning long-term residency, home ownership, retirement, or schooling.
- You want advice that integrates tax, legal, and lifestyle realities.

PROGRESS OVER PERFECTION

It's okay, and often smart, to start broad. But once your relocation becomes real, depth matters more than breadth. Realistically, you will probably end up working with more than one professional over time because specialist knowledge in the cross-border space is essential.

You don't need a perfect portfolio on day one, or even day 1,000. What matters is the following:

- Your strategy is intentional.
- Your costs are controlled.

- Your risks are understood.
- Your portfolio can move with you.
- You stay open to learning as your life evolves.

Whether you start with ETFs, move into direct indexing, or eventually work with a professional, the goal is the same: Build wealth that supports the life you're actually living, wherever in the world that may be.

PART IV

LIFE, FAMILY, AND THE LONG GAME

CHAPTER NINE

HOW DO I GET HEALTHCARE ABROAD?

Key Question: What are my healthcare options as an expat?

For a growing number of Americans, healthcare isn't just a logistical question when moving abroad; it's one of the main reasons they're considering leaving in the first place.

Rising costs, opaque billing, limited access to care, and employer-tied insurance have pushed many Americans to ask a once-uncomfortable question: Is there a better healthcare system somewhere else?

And in many cases, the honest answer is **yes**.

Across much of the developed world outside the United States, Americans are often surprised to find

- lower out-of-pocket costs for treatment and medications,
- easier access to primary care and specialists,
- transparent pricing, and

- strong public and private healthcare systems that aren't tied to employment.

Still, it's important to recognize one critical truth: Healthcare abroad is not universally "better."

It is highly dependent on where you go, what your healthcare needs will be, and how you plan to access care.

In other words: Moving abroad doesn't automatically fix healthcare woes. Choosing the right country and the right system within that country is what makes the difference.

Just as healthcare varies wildly from one US state to another, it varies even more dramatically from country to country. A move to Germany, Canada, or Japan creates a very different healthcare experience than a move to Mexico, Thailand, or Portugal. And those experiences differ from countries with limited infrastructure or underfunded public systems.

This chapter will help you understand the following:

- using US-based coverage abroad
- how public and private healthcare systems work abroad
- when international or global insurance makes sense and when it doesn't
- how to choose coverage that fits your life, not just your desired level of paperwork

You don't need to become an expert in global healthcare policy. You just need a framework that helps you make deliberate, informed decisions as your expat life evolves.

Bear in mind that even if your goal in moving abroad is simply just to leave the United States, you'll still need to land somewhere that supports your health, your finances, and your long-term quality of life.

Healthcare planning for expats ultimately comes down to one simple question: **"If I needed care tomorrow, who would treat me, and how much would it cost?"**

Everything in this chapter builds from the answer to that question.

SECTION 1: YOUR US HEALTH INSURANCE WILL NOT TRAVEL WITH YOU (AND THAT MATTERS)

One common and costly assumption Americans make when moving abroad is this: "I have good US health insurance, so I'll be fine for a while."

In most cases, that assumption is wrong.

Even excellent US health insurance plans provide little to no coverage outside the United States. Some offer limited emergency benefits abroad, but these are often tightly capped, reimbursed only after the fact, or subject to narrow definitions of what qualifies as an "emergency" (i.e., true life or death situations). Even then, coverage may only apply when you are "traveling," which is not entirely accurate when you have moved your life abroad.

That means that the moment you leave the United States, even temporarily, your healthcare safety net may disappear.

US Health Insurance and International Coverage: The Reality

Most US-based health plans fall into one of the following categories when you're abroad:

- **No coverage at all**
- **Emergency-only coverage**
  - With low lifetime or per-incident caps
  - Requiring you to pay up front and seek reimbursement later
  - Limited to short time frames (e.g., first 30–60 days abroad)

- Limited covered in specific countries or specific hospitals
- Coverage that excludes routine care, prescriptions, and follow-up treatment

Even if your plan technically covers emergencies abroad, it often does not provide the kind of access, clarity, or affordability people expect. As such, you will likely be personally on the hook for any incurred healthcare expenses abroad.

Keep in mind that emergency coverage is not the same as healthcare access. Preventative care, check-ups, and treatment for minor emergencies (e.g., infections requiring antibiotics, accidents where your life is not endangered) are important to take care of in order to keep you healthy, productive, and happy in your new home. **Typically, these are services provided or coordinated by a physician or a practice that you visit somewhat regularly, who will almost certainly require that you have valid insurance prior to scheduling or providing treatment**. So even if you have emergency coverage for a period from your US health insurance, these events will not be covered.

Scouting Trips, Exploratory Moves, and "We're Just Checking It Out"

Even if you're abroad on a short-term basis, a scouting trip, a trial stay, or an extended visit that doesn't require a visa, healthcare coverage still matters. Accidents don't wait for residency permits, and illness doesn't care whether your stay is "temporary." In many countries, hospitals will ask for proof of insurance or payment before providing care, and your US plan may deny reimbursement if its international coverage rules aren't followed precisely.

For these shorter stays, travel medical insurance is often the right solution. It's designed to cover emergencies and urgent care abroad, can include medical evacuation if needed, and provides a financial safety net while you explore whether a longer-term move makes sense. Before traveling, make sure that you understand the terms, conditions, and limits for your policy. Be aware that most plans are reimbursement-based, meaning that you may be forced to pay all expenses out-of-pocket before you are released from the hospital.

Travel insurance isn't meant to replace long-term healthcare, but it can prevent a bad situation from becoming financially catastrophic.

SECTION 2: HOW PUBLIC AND PRIVATE HEALTHCARE SYSTEMS WORK ABROAD

In the United States, healthcare tends to feel binary. You either have insurance, or you don't. You're either in-network or brace yourself for the bill. Abroad, healthcare usually works very differently, starting with the fact that *healthcare coverage is often compulsory.*

One of the biggest mindset shifts Americans face abroad is realizing that healthcare is no longer a single system with one clear entry point. In most countries, healthcare is built on **a public foundation**, with **private care layered on top**. Expats don't always choose one forever. They move between the two depending on eligibility, language, timing, and stage of life.

Understanding how these systems work together, and where the traps are, is what turns healthcare abroad from overwhelming into manageable.

Public Healthcare: Not Always Automatic

In much of the world, public healthcare is not a fallback for people who "can't afford better" or don't have employers that offer healthcare benefits. It's the system most people rely on, including professionals, families, and retirees.

Public healthcare is typically funded through taxes or mandatory social insurance contributions and is tied to legal residency, not employment. In some countries, public insurance is required by law, and the basic coverage is spelled out by regulation, but the choice of insurance company and premium payments are the responsibility of the policyholder. Once enrolled, coverage is often comprehensive: primary care, hospital stays, emergency treatment, and specialist care, usually with relatively low out-of-pocket costs.

For Americans, the first surprise is often how little money changes hands at the point of care. You see a doctor, present your insurance card, receive treatment, and leave without itemized bills or insurance negotiations. The second (less pleasant) surprise is that public healthcare isn't always fast. Nonurgent procedures may involve waiting periods, referrals are commonly required, and you may have less freedom to choose specific providers.

That trade-off is intentional. Public systems prioritize broad access, long-term sustainability, and cost control over speed and convenience. In countries with strong infrastructure, such as the United Kingdom, Germany, France, Japan, Canada, or Australia, this model works extremely well for emergencies, chronic conditions, and long-term care. But it can feel frustrating if you're used to immediate access or don't want to share a room during an inpatient hospital treatment.

It's also important to know that access to public healthcare is not always automatic, especially if you're moving as a retiree or as a self-employed individual. Partly to combat "healthcare tourism," many countries require proof of income, residency status, or specific contributions before allowing enrollment. Some visas require private insurance precisely because public enrollment isn't available right away, or at all.

This is why speaking with a local insurance or relocation expert before you move is essential. Each country has its own rules, and assumptions here can lead to higher-than-anticipated expenses or gaps in coverage.

Private Healthcare: When Access, Speed, and Language Matter

Private healthcare exists in nearly every country, even those with strong public systems. It doesn't replace public care so much as smooths the access points.

Private clinics and hospitals usually offer faster appointments, shorter wait times for diagnostics or elective procedures, private inpatient rooms, and greater flexibility in choosing providers. You may also have expanded access to alternative healthcare and wellness treatments. In many expat-heavy regions, private facilities also offer care in English, a detail that becomes far more important when you're sick, in pain, or navigating an unfamiliar system.

Another surprise for Americans is the cost. Private care abroad is often dramatically more affordable than in the United States. Services that might cost thousands of dollars stateside are frequently a few hundred dollars, sometimes less, when paid out of pocket abroad.

Because of this, many expats adopt a hybrid approach: relying on public healthcare for hospitalizations and major care, while using private providers for specialists, imaging, and routine needs. These so-called "semi-private" options offer a great compromise between access to quality and affordability.

Travel or private insurance can also act as a bridge, helping you access care before public enrollment is finalized or making the system easier to navigate if you don't speak the local language. Providers are often financially incentivized to accept private insurance, and private facilities may be more welcoming to nonnative speakers.

A Critical Warning About Opting Out

Here's a nuance many expats don't learn until it's too late: in some countries, fully opting out of the public system in favor of private insurance is a one-way door.

Public healthcare premiums are often income-based and relatively stable over time. Private insurance, on the other hand, is priced based on age and health. It can be inexpensive for young, healthy individuals, but premiums often rise sharply as you age and may become prohibitively expensive or even unavailable for anyone with preexisting conditions.

In certain systems, once you've chosen private insurance exclusively, you may not be allowed to re-enter the public system later. That can create serious long-term risk, especially for people planning to age abroad.

This doesn't mean private insurance is a bad choice. It means it should be chosen intentionally, with a clear understanding of how it fits into your long-term plan, not just your first year abroad.

A better question than "Which system is better?" is "How do I build healthcare access that works for my family and me now and still protects me as I age or move again?"

Once you understand how public and private systems interact, healthcare abroad becomes far less intimidating. In the next section, we'll look at how to choose insurance coverage, local, international, or temporary, that actually fits your life, not just your visa paperwork.

SECTION 3: WHEN INTERNATIONAL OR GLOBAL INSURANCE MAKES SENSE, AND WHEN IT DOESN'T

International health insurance is one of the most misunderstood parts of expat healthcare planning.

Some Americans assume it's the *gold standard* and buy the most expensive plan they can find "just to be safe." Others dismiss it entirely, assuming it's unnecessary once they move to a country with public healthcare. Both approaches miss the point.

International insurance is not inherently good or bad. It's a *tool*, and like any tool, it works best in specific situations and creates additional problems when used in the wrong ones.

The key question isn't, "Should I get international insurance?" but rather, "Does international insurance solve a real problem in my life right now, or am I paying for flexibility I don't actually need?"

What International Health Insurance Actually Is

International (or global) health insurance is designed for people who live outside their home country and may move across borders (potentially multiple times) within the policy period. Major insurers like Cigna Global, Allianz, and Aetna International typically offer these plans.

Unlike US health insurance, international plans have the following characteristics:

- Are not tied to an employer
- Are not tied to one specific country
- Usually allow you to receive care in multiple countries
- Often include evacuation and repatriation coverage

They are built for mobility, not permanence.

That distinction matters more than most people realize.

When International Insurance *Does* Make Sense

International insurance makes the most sense during periods of transition, when your life abroad is still taking shape and flexibility matters more than long-term efficiency. This is especially true if you're on a trial move, in the early stages of relocation, or on a limited/rotational expat assignment. Spending several months abroad to "test drive" a country or moving without a long-term visa in place can create uncertainty around residency and healthcare access. In these situations, international insurance can cover emergencies while you figure out what comes next, buying you time and peace of mind without prematurely locking you into a local system.

For people who move frequently or live a more nomadic lifestyle, international insurance provides continuity that local plans simply can't. If you don't know where you'll be next year, or even next month, having coverage that follows you across borders removes a significant layer of stress.

Language and access are other factors that play into international insurance. Early in a move, navigating a public healthcare system in a language you don't yet speak fluently—or even conversationally—can feel overwhelming, especially when you're sick or injured. International insurance frequently provides access to private clinics that cater to expats and operate in English, which can make a meaningful difference during already stressful moments. Finally, international insurance is one of the clearest ways to secure medical evacuation coverage. While evacuation is rarely needed, when it is, the costs can be staggering. For those living in countries with limited medical infrastructure, this feature alone can justify international coverage for a time.

When International Insurance Often *Doesn't* Make Sense

International insurance is not a forever solution for most expats, and in many cases, keeping it long-term is unnecessarily expensive. Once you're settled in a country where you qualify for public healthcare or a strong local private system, international coverage often becomes redundant. You may find yourself paying high premiums for benefits you rarely use while still relying on the local system for day-to-day care.

Cost is the biggest downside. International insurance is priced for flexibility and mobility, not efficiency. Premiums tend to be significantly higher than local plans, and they almost always increase with age. For younger, healthy individuals, this can feel manageable at first, but over time, the math becomes harder to justify, especially when comparable care is available locally at a fraction of the cost.

International insurance also doesn't integrate well with public systems. In many countries, you can't "blend" international coverage with public healthcare in a meaningful way. You may still be required to contribute to the public system through taxes or social insurance, even if you never use it.

That means you're effectively paying twice: once for access you don't use, and once for insurance designed for situations you no longer face.

Another limitation is longevity. International plans are not designed to be lifelong healthcare solutions. Coverage can change, premiums can spike, and underwriting rules may become stricter as you age or develop medical conditions. In contrast, public healthcare systems tend to offer stability and predictability over time, which becomes more important as healthcare needs increase.

For long-term residents, retirees, or anyone planning to build a permanent life in one country, international insurance is usually best viewed as a temporary tool rather than a permanent strategy. The goal is often to use it as a bridge, then transition thoughtfully into a local system that aligns better with both your healthcare needs and your long-term finances.

A Common (and Smart) Hybrid Approach

Experienced expats don't treat international insurance as a permanent solution. They use it strategically. A common and practical path looks like this: international insurance during the first year or two abroad, a transition into the public healthcare system when available, and then selective use of local private insurance or paying privately for faster access or English-speaking care.

This approach balances early flexibility with long-term affordability and stability. It also reflects how healthcare is actually used in many countries by locals and expats alike.

In the next section, we'll get practical: how to manage prescriptions, medical records, and continuity of care so your healthcare doesn't reset every time you cross a border.

SECTION 4: HOW TO CHOOSE COVERAGE THAT FITS YOUR LIFE (NOT JUST YOUR PAPERWORK)

One of the most common healthcare mistakes expats make is optimizing for paperwork instead of people.

They buy whatever insurance satisfies a visa requirement, enroll in whatever system is easiest and cheapest at the moment, and assume they'll sort out "real healthcare" later. The problem is that later often arrives in the form of illness or injury, exactly when you don't want to be figuring this out from scratch.

Good healthcare planning abroad isn't about finding *the best* plan on paper. It's about choosing coverage that works with how you actually live, move, age, and access care over time.

Start with Reality, Not Policy Language

Before comparing plans, take an honest look at how you use healthcare today.

Are you generally healthy and mostly need routine care? Do you manage a chronic condition? Do you rely on specific prescriptions, mental health support, or specialist care?

The "right" healthcare setup for a healthy 28-year-old on a trial move is very different from what works for a 45-year-old freelancer, a family with kids, or a retiree splitting time between countries. No insurance plan is universally good or bad; it's only good or bad *for you.*

Prescriptions: Plan for Continuity

Medications that are routine in the United States may be unavailable, prescribed differently, or regulated more tightly elsewhere. Brand names change. Dosages and availability per medication can differ. Some drugs that require a prescription in the United States are over the counter abroad (and vice versa), while others require a specialist.

Before you move, confirm the following:

- Whether your medication is available locally
- Whether the formulation and dosage are equivalent
- What type of doctor can prescribe it

Traveling with a buffer supply and a doctor's letter explaining your diagnosis and treatment plan can make the transition far smoother while you establish local care.

Medical Records: Build Your Own Portable System

Assume that healthcare systems will not talk to each other because they usually don't.

If you move countries, your new providers will almost never have access to your past records. That means you need to be the keeper of your own medical history.

Maintain secure digital copies of the following:

- Major diagnoses and surgeries
- Lab results and imaging reports
- Vaccination records

- Prescription histories
- Ongoing treatment plans

Vaccination records are particularly important if you are moving school-aged children. Each country maintains its own schedule of compulsory vaccinations. Not having this up-to-date documentation may subject your children to unnecessary and unpleasant needle sticks for vaccinations they have already received!

Choose Coverage That Can Evolve

Healthcare coverage abroad should not be a forever decision, especially one made in your first year.

Many expats use a layered approach over time: international insurance during early uncertainty, public healthcare once eligible, and private insurance as a supplement. What matters is flexibility. If your coverage allows you to adjust as your residency status, health, or location changes, you've chosen well.

The goal is not to insure against every possible outcome. It's to avoid locking yourself into a structure that becomes unaffordable, inaccessible, or limiting later.

Pro Tip

- With the exception of your initial enrollment on arrival, most countries allow you to change insurance providers once per calendar year and within a specific time window. If you plan to change your insurance, mark your calendar and set reminders so that you do not miss your chance!

SECTION 5: NOTES ON MEDICARE

Understand Medicare Early (Especially if You're Mid-career or Retired)

Medicare is one of the most common surprises for Americans abroad.

Key points to confirm:

- Medicare generally does *not* cover care outside the United States, with very limited exceptions.
- Many expats continue paying Medicare premiums while abroad, but receive little or no benefit.
- If you stop paying Medicare premiums and later return to the United States, you may face late enrollment penalties and coverage gaps.

If you think you may retire in the United States, even partially, confirm that you will meet the **10-year (40-quarter) US work requirement** needed to qualify for premium-free Medicare Part A. Many expats have split work histories and don't realize this requirement until it's difficult to fix.

This chapter can't cover every Medicare scenario, but it aims to surface common missteps early so you can engage the right professionals before decisions become permanent.

US Medicare for Retirees

Medicare is actually one of the strongest and most appealing retirement benefits provided by the US system, but retirees are often the most surprised by how little Medicare travels. After paying into the system for decades, and often continuing to pay monthly premiums, many assume Medicare will follow them abroad, at least in some meaningful way. In reality, it usually doesn't.

With very narrow exceptions involving border areas in Canada or Mexico, Medicare does not cover healthcare outside the United States. For most retirees living abroad, that means routine care, specialists, hospital stays, and prescriptions are entirely out of pocket unless separate coverage is in place. Medicare Advantage plans, which sometimes advertise limited international benefits, often impose strict caps, exclusions, or reimbursement hurdles that make them unreliable as a primary solution overseas.

This creates a frustrating disconnect. You may still be paying Medicare premiums every month and yet are receiving little to no benefit from the coverage while you're abroad. As a result, enrolling in a local healthcare system or securing international insurance becomes essential for retirees living outside the United States.

What Happens if You Stop Paying Medicare While Abroad?

Some retirees consider dropping Medicare Part B (and sometimes Part D) while living overseas, reasoning that it doesn't provide meaningful coverage abroad anyway. This can be a reasonable strategy in certain situations, but it comes with consequences that need to be understood up front.

If you stop paying Medicare Part B premiums and later return to the United States, you generally cannot re-enroll immediately. Instead, you must wait for the General Enrollment Period (January 1–March 31), with coverage starting July 1. Even more important, you may also face a permanent late enrollment penalty: your Part B premium increases by 10% for every full 12-month period you were eligible but not enrolled, and that higher premium lasts for life.

Part D prescription coverage carries similar penalties for late enrollment, while Part A is often premium-free for those who qualify, so dropping it is less common and usually unnecessary.

Stopping Medicare payments can save money while you're abroad, but it's not a neutral decision. If you do return to the United States, it trades short-term savings for higher long-term costs and delayed access. This decision should always be made intentionally, with a clear understanding of your likelihood of returning and your alternative healthcare coverage in the meantime.

For retirees abroad, Medicare isn't a safety net you can rely on internationally. It's a system you either plan around carefully or risk being caught off guard by later penalties and gaps in coverage.

A Note on Eligibility: Split Careers and the 10-year Rule

Another Medicare surprise many US expats don't see coming has nothing to do with coverage abroad; it's eligibility in the first place.

To qualify for premium-free Medicare Part A, you generally need **40 quarters (about 10 years) of US work history** where Medicare taxes were paid. Many Americans who build long careers abroad, especially those who leave the United States early or spend decades working for foreign employers, end up with **split work records** that fall short of this requirement.

This often takes people by surprise, catches people off guard when they begin planning retirement and realize the following:

- Their assumption that Medicare eligibility was automatic was incorrect.
- They stopped paying into the US system years earlier.
- Their foreign work history does not count toward Medicare eligibility.

If you don't meet the 40-quarter threshold, you may still be able to enroll in Medicare, but you'll likely face **significant monthly premiums** for Part A on top of Part B and Part D premiums. Over a long retirement, that can materially change your healthcare costs in the United States.

This matters even for expats who plan to retire abroad.

Many globally mobile Americans envision a **split retirement**: part of the year overseas, part of the year in the United States, or a later-life return for family, healthcare, or lifestyle reasons. In those scenarios, preserving Medicare eligibility, or at least understanding where you stand, becomes a long-term planning issue, not a last-minute checkbox at age 65.

We're Flagging This for You

This chapter cannot cover every Medicare planning strategy, exception, or edge case. The goal is to highlight **common missteps early**, while there is still time to fix them:

- Evaluate your US work record.
- Decide whether additional US employment or self-employment makes sense.
- Coordinate healthcare planning with tax, retirement, and residency decisions.

Medicare planning for US expats sits at the intersection of healthcare, taxation, and retirement strategy. That intersection is exactly where generic advice breaks down and where working with the right professionals becomes essential.

If this section raises questions for you, that's a feature, not a failure. It's a signal to engage with a US expat tax professional, a cross-border financial planner, or a Medicare specialist who understands globally mobile lives, before your options narrow.

SECTION 6: EXPAT HEALTHCARE—BEFORE AND AFTER YOU MOVE

The first step is to review your existing US coverage, don't assume it travels. Start by understanding what your current US health insurance does and does not cover once you leave the country.

Many US plans offer little to no international coverage or only cover emergencies under very specific conditions. Confirm the following:

- Whether coverage applies abroad at all
- How long coverage lasts outside the United States
- Whether reimbursement is required or providers must bill directly
- What exclusions could invalidate a claim

If you're planning scouting trips, trial stays, or extended visits without a visa, confirm whether travel medical insurance is appropriate. Even short stays can create real healthcare exposure.

Use Your US Benefits While You Still Have Them

If you currently have strong US coverage, this is one of the most overlooked opportunities in expat planning. Before leaving the United States, consider intentionally using benefits that may be harder, slower, or more expensive to access abroad:

- Schedule a full physical and preventive screenings.
- Visit specialists you've been putting off (dermatology, orthopedics, OB/GYN, etc.).

- Use vision and dental benefits (eye exams, glasses, contacts, dental work).
- Refill prescriptions and ask about extended supplies.
- Address chronic or "monitoring" issues while continuity of care is easy.
- Get copies of all medical records.
- Review vaccination records and request any vaccinations that may be recommended for the countries you will be traveling to.

Build a Portable Medical File

Before you move, gather and digitize all the following:

- A brief medical summary (conditions, allergies, ongoing treatments)
- Prescription lists with complete drug names
- Recent lab results and imaging
- Vaccination records

Store copies securely and keep a short, readable version you can share with new providers. This is especially important if you'll be navigating care in another language or healthcare system.

Research Healthcare in Your Destination Country

Healthcare abroad is highly location dependent.

Before moving, do all the following:

- Confirm the required healthcare coverage for your visa type.
- Understand whether healthcare is primarily public, private, or hybrid.

- Confirm whether access to public healthcare depends on employment, residency, or contributions.
- Connect with a local insurance or international healthcare expert.
- Understand whether opting out of the public system limits your ability to rejoin later.

Dental and vision coverage deserve special attention because they are rarely bundled into healthcare abroad the way Americans expect.

In many countries, dental care is not automatically included in public healthcare systems, and when it is, coverage may be limited to basic or emergency treatment. Comprehensive dental coverage is often handled separately, either through private insurance or out-of-pocket payment. Some private dental plans require an initial screening during enrollment, which can result in exclusions for preexisting conditions, waiting periods before coverage begins, or limits on major procedures. This means that ongoing dental issues or deferred work may not be covered under your new policy.

Vision care is similarly fragmented. Public systems may cover eye exams only under specific circumstances (such as medical necessity rather than routine vision correction), and private plans often provide only partial coverage for exams, lenses, or frames. Even where vision care is affordable out of pocket, coverage limits and reimbursement rules can differ sharply from what Americans are used to.

Before you move, confirm

- whether dental and vision care are included in the public system,
- whether separate private coverage is common or recommended, and
- what waiting periods or exclusions apply.

Depending on the answers, consider whether it might make sense to complete major dental or vision work while you still have US coverage.

Don't Forget HSAs and FSAs: Healthcare Accounts Don't Always Travel Well

Health Savings Accounts (HSAs) and Flexible Spending Accounts (FSAs) are powerful tools within the US financial and healthcare systems, but their tax advantages are largely US-specific.

While HSAs enjoy triple tax benefits in the United States (tax-deductible contributions, tax-deferred growth, and tax-free withdrawals for qualified medical expenses), most foreign tax systems do not recognize this structure. Once you become a tax resident abroad, your HSA may be treated like a regular investment or savings account. That means interest, dividends, or capital gains inside the account can become currently taxable in your country of residence, especially if the funds are invested for long-term growth.

FSAs are even less portable as they are typically tied to US employment and subject to "use-it-or-lose-it" rules. If you're planning a move, make sure you understand your employer's deadlines and spend eligible funds before you lose access.

HSAs can still be valuable long-term, particularly if you plan to return to the United States or use them later for US-based medical expenses. But once you move abroad, they should be reviewed as part of your broader tax and healthcare planning, not treated as a set-it-and-forget-it account.

AFTER YOU ARRIVE

Once you've arrived, enroll in the public healthcare system as soon as you're eligible and take time to understand how it actually works. Confirm required contributions, how primary care and specialist referrals function, and whether there is a waiting period before coverage begins.

If there's a gap, international or local private insurance can serve as a temporary bridge.

Establish Access Points Early

Once settled, be sure to do the following:

- Identify a primary care doctor or clinic that is accepting new patients (and visit them!).
- Locate English-speaking providers if language is a concern.
- Understand how prescriptions are issued and refilled locally.
- Confirm emergency procedures and the nearest hospitals.

Don't wait until you're sick or injured to figure out how the system works.

Reassess Coverage Over Time

Healthcare planning isn't static.

Revisit your setup:

- Annually
- After a job change
- When residency status changes
- After a major relocation
- As you age or develop new health considerations

What made sense during your first year abroad may not make sense five years later, and that's normal.

Healthcare abroad doesn't have to be perfect to be good; it just needs to be intentional. The biggest mistakes expats make aren't about choosing the "wrong" system; they're about assuming healthcare will sort itself out. A bit of planning before you move, and periodic recalibration after you arrive, can prevent unnecessary stress, surprise expenses, and long-term regret.

US healthcare coverage is designed for life inside the US system. Once you step outside that system, even briefly, you need to make conscious choices about how you'll access care, who will pay for it, and what happens in an emergency. That doesn't mean moving abroad is risky. It means assuming coverage without confirming it is. The goal isn't to replicate US healthcare somewhere else, but to build coverage that actually supports your life, wherever that life takes you next.

Quick Healthcare Reality Checklist

Before You Move

- Confirm what your US health insurance *actually* covers abroad (if anything)
- If you are retired, don't assume Medicare travels, understand coverage, premiums, and penalties
- Use US benefits while you still have them (checkups, dental, vision, prescriptions)
- Digitize medical records, prescriptions, and vaccination history
- Research public vs. private healthcare in your destination country
- Confirm dental and vision coverage separately
- Review HSAs/FSAs—tax treatment may change once you're abroad.

After You Arrive

- Enroll in public healthcare as soon as eligible
- Use international or private insurance as a bridge if needed
- Establish a primary care doctor and understand emergency procedures
- Reassess coverage annually or after major life changes

CHAPTER TEN

WHAT HAPPENS TO MY ESTATE IF I LIVE (OR DIE) ABROAD?

Key Question: What happens to my assets, my family, and my decisions if I live or die abroad?

For most Americans, estate planning is something you do once, file away, and hope you won't need for a very long time. You write a will, name beneficiaries, maybe set up a trust, and move on with life.

When you cross borders, though, estate planning stops being a one-country exercise. The rules that govern who inherits, how assets are taxed, which documents are recognized, and even who counts as "family" can change, sometimes dramatically, based on where you live, where your assets are located, and where your heirs reside.

The estate plan that worked perfectly in the United States may no longer work the way you expect once another legal system is involved. Many Americans incorrectly assume estate planning is only about death. In reality, international estate planning is just as much about life, protecting a spouse, partner, or children while you're living abroad; ensuring someone can act on your behalf if you're incapacitated; and avoiding legal or tax complications that can affect your family long before an estate is ever settled.

For US citizens, the complexity multiplies quickly. As we've discussed, the United States taxes its citizens based on citizenship, not residence. Many other countries tax estates or inheritances based on residency, domicile, or the location of assets. These systems don't align neatly, and in some cases, they don't align at all.

When people hear "international estate planning," they usually think about taxes first. Estate tax. Inheritance tax. Double taxation.

Taxes are often not the first thing that breaks when someone moves abroad.

More often, the problems start with much more basic and personal questions:

- Is my spouse legally recognized here?
- Are my children considered heirs under local law?
- Can I leave assets the way I want, or does the country I live in decide for me?
- Does my US trust still function as a trust abroad?
- What about a trust my parents set up for my children or me? Does that still work the same way?
- Will my power of attorney or healthcare directive even be accepted?

You can see why estate planning becomes one of the most misunderstood, most emotionally charged, and potentially complex topics for Americans living abroad.

The next few chapters are not meant to turn you into an estate planning or family law expert. It's meant to give you a framework for understanding where problems commonly arise, what questions to ask, and when it's time to involve the right professionals who understand cross-border lives.

You do not need to have a large estate for this to matter. Even modest assets can trigger significant tax, legal, or administrative complications when they cross borders. And some of the highest impact risks, like non-recognition of a spouse, child, or decision-maker, have nothing to do with wealth at all.

Throughout these chapters, we'll focus on the realities that most often surprise Americans abroad:

- How estate and inheritance taxes differ across countries
- Why residence, domicile, and asset location matter more than intent
- When US estate planning tools work internationally, and when they don't
- How family structures can be treated differently across legal systems
- Why planning for incapacity is just as important as planning for death

Just as with healthcare, taxes, and housing, estate planning abroad isn't about perfection. It's about intentionality. Intentional plans are the ones that acknowledge complexity early, adapt to local realities, and protect the people you care about across borders.

In the chapters that follow, we'll break down the concepts you need to understand, the traps to avoid, and the conversations worth having, so your international life doesn't leave your family navigating a maze with no solution.

CHAPTER ELEVEN

WHO COUNTS AS FAMILY? MARRIAGE AND OWNERSHIP ACROSS BORDERS

Key Question: How are my relationships, my family, and my rights treated across different legal systems, and what happens if they don't align?

In the United States, most people assume family status is straightforward. A spouse is a spouse. Children are children. Divorce is final. Adoption is permanent. These definitions feel settled, definite. Living abroad, however, can cause complications.

Family law can be extremely local. Each country defines relationships, parental rights, marital status, and inheritance differently. And when more than one legal system is involved, those definitions don't always line up or even recognize each other.

For Americans living abroad, this creates a surprising risk: your legal family in one country may not be your legal family in another. That gap can affect immigration considerations, inheritance rights, decision-making authority, tax exposure, and even access to assets in an emergency.

This chapter isn't about extreme cases or rare situations. It's about common family structures that Americans take for granted and how they can be treated very differently once borders are involved.

MARRIAGE IS NOT AS UNIVERSAL AS IT FEELS

Marriage often feels like the most universally recognized legal relationship. In international estate planning, it is frequently the first place where assumptions need to be pressure-tested against local rules.

Different countries recognize marriage differently, especially when it comes to the following:

- Same-sex marriage
- Marriages performed abroad
- Marriages entered into after divorce
- Religious or customary marriages
- Civil partnerships or registered partnerships

Even when a marriage is valid in the United States, another country may require additional steps, such as registration, formal recognition, or specific documentation, before it is treated as legally binding. Without completing those steps, a surviving spouse may not be recognized as a spouse at all for inheritance, tax, or property purposes.

For same-sex couples, the risk can be even higher. While legal recognition has expanded significantly, it is still not universal. Some countries recognize same-sex marriages fully, others partially, and some not at all. That difference can determine whether a partner inherits automatically, qualifies for spousal tax exemptions, or has legal authority to act on behalf of an incapacitated spouse.

> **Expat Insight:** *In parts of the Middle East and North Africa, including the UAE, Qatar, Saudi Arabia, and Egypt, same-sex relationships are not legally recognized, and in some cases are criminalized. Similar risks exist in countries such as Nigeria and parts of Southeast Asia.*
>
> *Even in countries where same-sex relationships are not criminalized, legal recognition may still be limited. For example, Japan does not recognize same-sex marriage at the national level, though some municipalities offer partnership certificates with limited legal effect. In parts of Europe, including Poland and Ukraine, recognition is also limited or nonexistent. Other countries, such as Italy or Greece, offer civil unions that provide some legal rights, but not the full protections of marriage.*
>
> *— Arielle Tucker, CFP®, EA, Passport To Wealth™*

INFORMAL RELATIONSHIPS AND COMMON-LAW MARRIAGE

Common-law marriage is recognized in some US states, but it is far from universally recognized internationally.

Many countries require formal registration of relationships to grant spousal rights. Living together, sharing finances, or presenting yourselves as a couple may carry little or no legal weight. In estate and inheritance contexts, this can mean no automatic inheritance rights, no spousal tax exemptions, and no authority to make medical or financial decisions.

Without documentation that is recognized locally, a surviving partner may have very limited protection, even after decades together.

RECOGNITION IS ONLY HALF THE STORY: OWNERSHIP MATTERS TOO

Even when a marriage *is* legally recognized, a second question quickly follows: What does that marriage actually mean for ownership of assets?

In the United States, many couples assume marriage does not automatically determine who owns what. Assets are often titled individually, and ownership can feel flexible. While this may be true in many US states, it is not how marriage works everywhere.

Around the world, marital property is governed by marital property regimes, legal systems that determine how assets are owned during marriage and divided at death or divorce. These regimes often apply automatically unless you have formally opted out, sometimes before marriage or upon establishing residency.

This creates another quiet but powerful risk for Americans abroad: you may be married to someone the law recognizes, but you may not own your assets the way you think you do.

COMMUNITY PROPERTY, SEPARATE PROPERTY, AND DEFAULT RULES

Some countries follow community-property-style regimes, where assets acquired during marriage are considered jointly owned regardless of whose name is on the account or deed. Others follow separate or equitable property systems, where ownership depends more on title, contribution, or contract.

The United States itself is split between these approaches. But many Americans living abroad unknowingly step into mandatory community property systems.

In countries such as France, Spain, Germany, Switzerland, and much of Latin America, marital property regimes are deeply embedded in family law. If no election is made, a default regime applies automatically, often based on where you lived when you married or where you establish residence later.

These regimes can override expectations formed under US law. Assets you thought were "yours" may already be considered jointly owned. A surviving spouse may be entitled to a portion of assets regardless of what your will says. Children from prior relationships may have claims you did not anticipate. Lifetime gifts, inheritances, or business interests may be treated very differently than expected.

In some systems, you cannot freely leave all assets to a spouse or children, even if your US estate plan says so. The marital property regime sets the starting point. Your estate plan often operates on top of it, not instead of it.

> **Expert Insights:** *If you hold assets in multiple jurisdictions, it is even more important than usual to consider what happens at death—not just legally, but from a tax perspective. Sweden abolished inheritance tax in 2005, but foreign trusts are a legal structure Swedish law does not directly recognize. Like many countries, Sweden has not adopted the Hague Trust Convention, so trust arrangements must instead be classified under domestic tax principles. Depending on how the trust deed is structured and who is considered to control the assets, distributions to Swedish-resident beneficiaries may be taxed as periodiskt understöd (periodic support) in the employment-income category—potentially subject to progressive taxation exceeding 50%, an outcome many US estate plans never anticipate.*
>
> *—Lori Nitzel*

MIXED FAMILIES, MIXED RULES

Complexity increases further when spouses have different nationalities, have lived in multiple countries over time, or hold assets in more than one jurisdiction.

Which country's marital property law applies is not always intuitive. It may depend on where you first established your marital residence, where you currently live, whether you signed a marital agreement, or whether you later moved to another country without updating your documentation.

As a result, a couple married in the United States, living abroad, with assets in both places, may be subject to multiple overlapping property concepts unless planning is coordinated intentionally.

PRENUPS, POSTNUPS, AND RECOGNITION RISK

Many Americans assume a US prenuptial or postnuptial agreement will automatically control outcomes abroad. Sometimes it helps. Sometimes it doesn't. Some countries do not recognize foreign marital agreements at all. Others require specific formalities or limit what spouses are allowed to contract around. An agreement that is perfectly valid in the United States may need to be reaffirmed, adapted, or re-executed locally to be effective.

DIVORCE, PRIOR MARRIAGES, AND "FINALITY"

Another common surprise is that divorce implications may be different depending on the country.

A divorce that is final and legally recognized in the United States may require formal recognition or validation in another country before it is respected under local law. Until that happens, a former spouse may still be treated as a legal spouse for certain purposes, including inheritance or marital property claims.

This matters enormously in estate planning. Without proper recognition, any of the following could happen:

- A former spouse could have inheritance rights you thought were extinguished.
- A current spouse could face challenges asserting their status.
- Children from prior relationships could be affected by competing claims.

These issues often surface only at death or incapacity, precisely when they are hardest to fix.

CHILDREN, STEPCHILDREN, AND ADOPTION ACROSS BORDERS

In the United States, adopted children generally have the same inheritance rights as biological children. Stepchildren often inherit if named in a will or trust. These assumptions do not hold everywhere.

Countries may draw their own legal distinctions among

- biological children,
- adopted children, and
- stepchildren.

In most jurisdictions, stepchildren have no automatic inheritance rights at all, even if they were raised by the deceased and treated as family in every practical sense. Without explicit planning that complies with local law, a stepchild may be entirely excluded from an estate.

Adoption can also become more complicated across borders. An adoption completed in the United States may need to be formally recognized or re-registered in the country of residence before it is fully respected for inheritance purposes. Without that recognition, an adopted child may not qualify as a legal heir under local law.

In countries with forced heirship rules, the distinction becomes even more significant. Forced heirship laws require that a portion of an estate pass to certain legally defined heirs, often limited to biological or formally adopted children. For families with blended structures, international moves can unintentionally disinherit children unless planning is updated intentionally and locally.

WHY THIS MATTERS *BEFORE* TAXES ENTER THE PICTURE

Before estate or inheritance taxes ever apply, someone must be recognized as an heir.

If a spouse, partner, or child is not legally recognized under local law, they may

- not inherit automatically,
- face higher tax rates or lower exemptions,
- need to litigate to assert rights, or
- be excluded entirely.

This is why international estate planning cannot start with tax optimization alone. The foundational question is legal recognition. Who does the law say your family is? And which law is being applied? Even when relationships are legally recognized, access to assets and decision-making authority does not always transfer as smoothly as people expect. Cross-border administration can create delays, restrictions, and unintended complications.

> **Expert Insight:** *Estate planning becomes especially important when living abroad, not just for tax reasons, but to ensure the right people can act and access assets when needed.*
>
> *Many families assume that assets held jointly or in a living trust will transfer immediately to a surviving spouse. While this is often true within the United States, the process can be significantly delayed when the account holder lives abroad.*

(*Continued*)

(Continued)

> *In many cases, custodians restrict trading and withdrawals until they receive an IRS Transfer Certificate confirming that any US estate tax obligations have been addressed. Obtaining this certificate can take months or even over a year.*
>
> *During that time, a surviving spouse may have limited or no access to funds.*
>
> *In situations where health is declining or a transition is anticipated, having assets titled in the other spouse's name or ensuring access to liquid funds can make a meaningful difference. Planning ahead can help ensure that a surviving partner is not left navigating administrative delays without financial access.*
>
> *Similar complications can arise during divorce. Accounts may be temporarily restricted until proper legal documentation is received and processed. For US-based retirement plans, dividing assets often requires a Qualified Domestic Relations Order (QDRO), even when the divorce occurs abroad.*
>
> *These processes can take longer and become more complex when multiple legal systems are involved, reinforcing the importance of coordinating family, legal, and financial structures across borders.*
>
> *—Otto Rivera, CFP®, EA, Mindful Wealth*

THE PRACTICAL TAKEAWAY

If you live abroad, or expect to, estate planning starts with validating assumptions you didn't even know you were making.

It means confirming the following:

- That your marriage is recognized where you live
- That prior divorces are legally final in all relevant jurisdictions
- That your children are recognized as heirs under local law
- That your partner has legal standing if something happens to you

These are not theoretical concerns. They are the issues that most often create disputes, delays, and heartbreak for international families.

CHAPTER TWELVE

CAN I LEAVE MY ASSETS TO WHOMEVER I WANT?

FORCED HEIRSHIP, TREATIES, AND THE LIMITS OF CHOICE ABROAD

For many Americans, estate planning starts from a place of confidence: If I write a will, I get to decide who inherits my assets.

In the United States, that assumption is generally correct. Outside of a few narrow protections, US law prioritizes testamentary freedom. Your will reflects your intent, and the legal system is designed to carry it out.

Living abroad can significantly curb these freedoms without careful advance planning.

In many countries, inheritance is not treated as a personal choice but as a family obligation. The law may dictate who must inherit, how much they must receive, and how those transfers are taxed, regardless of what your US will says. These rules are known broadly as forced heirship and inheritance tax regimes, and they are one of the most significant departures from the US estate planning mindset.

This chapter explores where Americans still have flexibility, where that flexibility quietly disappears, and why even families with straightforward plans can be surprised once borders are involved.

ESTATE TAX TREATIES: A HELPFUL STARTING POINT (BUT NOT A FREE PASS)

The good news first: the United States does have estate and gift tax treaties with a limited number of countries, including several in Europe. Much like income tax treaties, the function of estate is covered. These treaties are to reduce double taxation and, in some cases, clarify which country has primary taxing rights over certain assets.

If you are

- a US citizen
- living abroad
- with no local citizenship
- and your heirs are US persons,

you may still retain a meaningful degree of control over who receives your estate, particularly from a US estate tax perspective.

But this is where many expats stop digging and where problems can accumulate and fester.

Estate tax treaties are narrow in scope. They do not override local inheritance law, forced heirship rules, or family law definitions. They also do not necessarily protect heirs from local inheritance taxes, even when assets are entirely US-based.

Treaties can help coordinate taxation. They do not eliminate complexity.

> **Expert Insight:** *For some reason, many clients feel the need to update their estate plan in the United States BEFORE they expatriate. That is not the case! Rarely will a US-based estate plan work well in a foreign jurisdiction, particularly in my area of expertise—Canada. Powers of attorney are very specific to each state/province, a US will likely has provisions that are unenforceable in a foreign jurisdiction, and courts and lawyers can tie up things for years when a US will or power of attorney is submitted to a foreign court.*
>
> *—Brian Wruk, MBA, CFP®(US), CFP®(Canada), TEP, CIM, RFP®,*
> *Transition Financial Advisors*

WHEN CHOICE STARTS TO SHRINK

Estate planning becomes significantly more complicated when one or more of the following applies:

- You are married to a non-US citizen.
- You have obtained citizenship in your country of residence.
- Your spouse or children are citizens or residents of that country.
- You own assets located outside the United States.
- You reside long term in a country with forced heirship rules.

Each of these factors can pull local law into the picture.

At that point, the question shifts from "What does my will say?" to "Which legal system gets to decide?"

And the answer is often: more than one.

FORCED HEIRSHIP: WHEN THE LAW DECIDES FOR YOU

Let's dive a bit deeper into this topic we've touched on a bit earlier. Forced heirship rules require that a portion of your estate pass to certain legally protected heirs, most commonly children, and sometimes spouses.

The portion you are free to distribute however you want may be limited. In some countries, it can be surprisingly small.

This applies even if the following are true:

- Your will was drafted in the United States.
- Your heirs live in the United States.
- You never intended local law to apply.

If local forced heirship rules are triggered, your will does not override them. It operates *within* them.

This is particularly impactful under the following circumstances:

- Blended families
- Second marriages
- Families with stepchildren
- Situations where one child is financially secure and another is not

Forced heirship is not about fairness as you define it. It's about statutory entitlement.

INHERITANCE TAX: THE SHOCK MANY EXPATS DON'T SEE COMING

One of the most common and emotionally charged surprises for Americans abroad has nothing to do with their own estate at all.

It's what happens when their parents or relatives in the United States pass away.

Many Americans living abroad are stunned to discover that they may owe inheritance tax in their country of residence on assets they inherit, even when the following are true:

- The deceased was not a citizen of that country.
- The assets were entirely US-based.
- The estate paid no US estate tax.
- The inheritance would have been tax-free if they had lived in the United States.

In many countries, inheritance tax is based on the heir's residence, not the deceased's citizenship. Simply living in that country can create a tax obligation on wealth you did not build there and assets that never touched that country.

This is a fundamental difference from the US system, where inheritance tax is rare and estate tax exemptions are high. For expats, this often feels deeply unfair and deeply unexpected.

TREATIES DON'T ALWAYS PROTECT HEIRS

Even where an estate or gift tax treaty exists, relief may be limited.

Why?

- The United States taxes estates; many countries tax heirs.
- Exemptions and rate structures don't align.
- Credits may be available in theory, but difficult to apply in practice.
- State-level taxes may not conform at all.

The result is that heirs may face real tax bills abroad with limited ability to offset them, even when everyone acted in good faith.

TRUSTS: POWERFUL AT HOME, FRAGILE ABROAD

Many Americans rely on trusts to control distributions, protect heirs, avoid probate, and reduce taxes. In the United States, trusts are flexible and well understood.

Abroad, misunderstanding how trusts are viewed in a local context can cause major headaches.

Some countries

- do not recognize trusts as separate legal entities,
- treat trust assets as still personally owned,
- tax trust income or gains annually, or
- ignore trusts entirely for forced heirship calculations.

In forced heirship jurisdictions, assets placed into a trust may still be pulled back into the estate when determining heirs' mandatory shares.

This doesn't mean trusts should never be used. It means they must be evaluated country by country, not assumed to function universally.

These rules don't just change tax outcomes. They change family dynamics. They can have distressing results:

- Override carefully considered intentions
- Reignite old family tensions
- Create unequal outcomes between children
- Surprise heirs with large tax bills
- Force legal disputes at the worst possible time

And because these issues often surface only at death, there is rarely an opportunity to fix them once they appear.

Expert Insight: *Many Americans relocate to France with a standard US estate plan built around a revocable living trust, assuming the structure will simply continue to function as intended.*

In reality, France does not recognize trusts in the same way the United States does.

This difference can create unexpected consequences once you become resident in France. Local authorities may not treat the trust as the effective owner of the assets. Instead, they may look through the structure and analyze the situation based on who created the trust, who controls it, and who benefits from it.

The result can be significant reporting obligations, legal uncertainty about asset ownership, and complications in the event of death if the structure is not properly understood in the local legal framework.

The mistake many families make is addressing these questions after they have already moved, often years later when filing tax returns, responding to compliance requests, or during a succession process.

(Continued)

(Continued)

> *Before relocating, it is essential to review any existing US estate planning structures with a professional familiar with both legal systems. In many cases, the trust itself does not need to be changed—but the way it is analyzed, documented, and reported must be carefully adapted to the country of residence.*
>
> *Cross-border estate planning is rarely about replacing structures. It is about making sure they remain coherent across jurisdictions.*
>
> *—Thomas Dubanchet, Bespoke Tax*

THE PRACTICAL TAKEAWAY

If you live abroad, the core estate planning question is not: "Do I have a will?"

It's: "Which laws will actually apply when it matters?"

US estate tax treaties can help, but they are not a shield against forced heirship, inheritance tax, or mismatched legal definitions of family. The moment non-US spouses, citizenships, residences, or heirs enter the picture, planning must become intentional and coordinated across borders.

In the next chapter, we'll explore how families try to plan around these constraints, what strategies can help, where they fall short, and how to reduce surprises for the people you care about most.

CHAPTER THIRTEEN

HOW DO I ACTUALLY BUILD A CROSS-BORDER ESTATE PLAN THAT WORKS?

Key Question: What steps do I need to take to ensure my will, assets, and family are protected across multiple legal systems?

At this point in the book, many readers arrive at the same moment of realization and the same question.

Okay, I understand the risks. But what do I actually do now?

This chapter is where international estate planning becomes practical, grounded in how real families plan around competing legal systems, imperfect tools, and global lives.

There is no single structure that "solves" cross-border estate planning. What works instead is coordination: understanding which rules apply, where flexibility exists, and how to reduce the likelihood that your family is left untangling legal contradictions when you're no longer there to explain them.

START WITH WHAT YOU ALREADY HAVE

Most Americans who move abroad don't start from zero. They already have *something* in place, a US will drafted years ago, beneficiary designations on brokerage and retirement accounts, maybe a trust created when children were born, and powers of attorney tucked into a folder that hasn't been opened in a decade.

The mistake isn't having these documents. The mistake is assuming they are either fully sufficient or completely invalid once you cross a border.

In reality, most international estate planning begins with a document audit. This document considers several questions:

- What exists?
- Where was it created?
- Which law governs it?
- And what assumptions does it make about family relationships, ownership, or legal concepts that may not exist where you now live?

This step alone often reveals issues that are relatively easy to fix while you're alive, and extremely difficult for your family to resolve later.

ONE WILL OR MULTIPLE WILLS? THERE'S NO DEFAULT ANSWER

One of the first structural questions expats encounter is whether they should have a single global will or separate wills for different countries.

A single will can feel cleaner. It centralizes intent and reduces the risk of contradictory instructions. But in some countries, local probate procedures, language requirements, or asset-specific rules make a local will more practical, especially for local real estate.

Multiple wills can speed administration and reduce friction, but only if they are carefully coordinated. A poorly drafted local will can unintentionally revoke a broader plan or override dispositions you never meant to change.

This isn't a choice to make based on convenience alone. It requires professionals who understand how documents interact across borders, not just within them. You will likely need to engage with an international estate attorney who will collaborate closely with your cross-border tax and financial planning (as applicable) team.

WHERE ASSETS LIVE STILL MATTERS, A LOT

Even in the context of a global life, assets remain stubbornly evaluated at the local level.

Real estate is governed by the law of the country where it sits. Some business interests, bank accounts, and pensions are similarly anchored. That means a US will may not fully control how a foreign property is transferred or whether local inheritance rules apply, regardless of your intent.

International planning starts by mapping not just *what* you own, but *where* it lives, and which legal system gets first say over its transfer. Ignoring asset location is one of the fastest ways to turn a straightforward estate into a multi-year administrative process.

TRUSTS ARE POWERFUL, BUT NOT PORTABLE

For Americans, trusts often feel like a default solution. They're flexible, familiar, and widely respected in the US legal system. Abroad, that familiarity disappears.

In many countries, trusts are not recognized in the same way or at all. Some jurisdictions recharacterize them. Others treat them as transparent. Some tax them aggressively year after year, even if no distributions are made.

This doesn't mean trusts should never be used. It means they need to be tested carefully against local tax rules, inheritance laws, and reporting requirements. The most dangerous assumption is that a trust "just works everywhere." It doesn't.

BENEFICIARY DESIGNATIONS CAN OVERRIDE EVERYTHING

One of the simplest estate planning tools is also one of the most powerful—and most often overlooked.

Beneficiary designations on retirement accounts, life insurance policies, and certain investment accounts frequently override what your will says entirely. In many cases, that's intentional and efficient. In others, it creates results you never anticipated, especially when international borders are involved.

In a cross-border context, beneficiary designations can bypass forced heirship rules, conflict with local inheritance laws, or trigger unexpected tax consequences for heirs who live outside the United States. A designation that works cleanly under US law may produce very different outcomes once a foreign legal or tax system applies.

This issue applies both ways. US citizens living abroad must think carefully about how beneficiary designations will be treated where their heirs live. At the same time, US-based individuals with foreign-resident beneficiaries often overlook the fact that those heirs may face inheritance taxes, reporting obligations, or restrictions in their country of residence, even when the underlying assets are entirely US-based.

Because beneficiary designations operate automatically, they deserve deliberate review. Aligning them with your broader estate plan and with the tax and legal realities your heirs will face is one of the highest impact, lowest effort steps you can take in international estate planning.

INCAPACITY PLANNING MATTERS EVEN MORE ABROAD

For families living abroad, planning for incapacity is often more urgent and more complicated.

Many countries do not automatically recognize US powers of attorney or healthcare directives. Others require local court involvement, government-approved forms, or formal registration before anyone can legally act on your behalf. That means if you become incapacitated abroad, your spouse or partner may not automatically be able to access bank accounts, manage property, make medical decisions, or advocate for your care, even if you have perfectly valid US documents.

For parents of young children, the stakes are even higher.

If something happens to you and your partner at the same time, local authorities will not "wait and see" who you would have wanted to step in. Without a clear, locally recognized plan, the state will decide where your children go, who has temporary custody, and how that transition happens. That decision may be driven by proximity and local law, not by your intentions or your children's existing relationships with unrelated parties.

This is where many international families benefit from naming local temporary guardians, even if their long-term guardians live in the United States or another country. A temporary guardian who is already in your country of residence can ensure your children go to a familiar, trusted person immediately, someone who can care for them, communicate with schools and doctors, and provide stability, while longer-term guardians make travel arrangements and legal steps are completed.

Just as important as the documents themselves is the conversation around them. Guardianship plans should never be a surprise. All parties—local temporary guardians, long-term guardians, and close family—should understand the plan, agree to their roles, and know what would happen in an emergency. International moves add another layer of complexity, so plans should be revisited if close friends relocate, family circumstances change, or your country of residence shifts.

Incapacity planning isn't pessimistic. It's an act of care. It ensures that if the unexpected happens, decisions are made by people you choose, in a way that protects your children, your partner, and your life across borders.

TREATIES HELP—BUT THEY DON'T SOLVE EVERYTHING

One of the first questions Americans abroad ask when estate planning comes up is whether there's a tax treaty that will "fix" the problem. Sometimes there is. Sometimes there isn't. And even when there is, it's rarely a complete solution on its own.

The United States has estate and gift tax treaties with a limited number of countries. When they apply, these treaties can be extremely valuable. They are designed to reduce or prevent double estate taxation by coordinating how two countries assert taxing rights over the same assets.

At their best, estate tax treaties can help determine which country has priority to tax, provide credits so that tax paid in one country offsets tax owed in another, and clarify how assets are classified for tax purposes. Many treaties also include tie-breaker rules to determine residency or domicile for estate tax purposes when more than one country could plausibly claim taxing authority. In some cases, they define where certain assets are considered "situated," which can materially change the amount of tax owed and where it is owed.

However, whether a treaty applies and how useful it actually is depends entirely on the facts. Treaties are highly specific. They look at the status of the decedent, the countries involved, the type and location of assets, and how each country defines concepts like residency or domicile. Two people living in the same country can have very different outcomes depending on citizenship, length of residence, or family circumstances.

It's also important to understand what happens when there is no treaty.

Many US expats live in countries that do not have estate tax treaties with the United States, including places like the UAE, Singapore, Hong Kong, Thailand, Malaysia, and Qatar. In these situations, there is no formal mechanism to coordinate the US estate tax system with local inheritance or estate tax rules.

That means US rules generally apply to the worldwide estate of a US citizen, while local rules may apply based on residency, domicile, or asset location. If both systems assert taxing rights, there may be no automatic credit or relief. The risk of double taxation is real, and planning options are often more limited.

Even when a treaty does exist, it's critical to understand what treaties do *not* do.

Estate tax treaties are tax agreements. They are not family law agreements. They do not harmonize legal systems or override local inheritance rules. A treaty will not eliminate forced heirship requirements. It will not guarantee that a US trust is recognized as a trust abroad. It will not fix mismatches in how spouses, children, or heirs are defined. And it will not ensure that your US estate planning documents are accepted or enforceable in another country.

Treaties are often discussed as if they were a safety net. In reality, they are a tool, one piece of a much larger planning puzzle. Used thoughtfully, they can reduce taxes and prevent unnecessary duplication. Used blindly, they can create a false sense of security.

The most effective international estate plans treat treaties as an overlay, not a foundation. They start with the legal realities of where you live, how your family is defined, and how assets are owned. Then, if a treaty applies, it's layered in to optimize the tax outcome—not relied on to solve structural issues it was never designed to address.

Treaties help provide context and clarity around options, particularly if you're not able to work ahead of a major event that calls the divvying up of an estate into question. But they don't replace intentional, cross-border planning.

FAMILY CONVERSATIONS MATTER MORE THAN ANY STRUCTURE

At a certain point, even the most carefully drafted legal structures reach their limits.

Cross-border estates are rarely tidy. Assets may sit in different countries. Heirs may live under different tax systems. One child may inherit tax-free, while another faces a meaningful inheritance tax bill simply because of where they live. No will, trust, or treaty can make those outcomes feel perfectly fair from every angle.

What *does* make a difference is communication.

Clear, honest conversations about intent, why things are structured the way they are, what constraints exist, and what trade-offs were unavoidable often prevent more conflict than any technical planning tool. Silence, on the other hand, rarely protects families. It usually shifts confusion, resentment, and hard decisions onto the people left behind.

For US expats, this is especially important when aging parents remain in the United States.

Many parents create estate plans assuming all children live in the same country and face the same rules. They may have no idea that a child living abroad could be subject to inheritance tax, reporting requirements, or administrative hurdles that don't exist for siblings back home, even when the assets are entirely US-based. The shock often comes *after* a parent's death, when there's no longer an opportunity to adjust the plan or explain the intent.

Starting these conversations early can change everything.

That doesn't mean turning family dinners into tax seminars. It can be as simple as asking some questions:

- Do you know that living abroad may affect how an inheritance is taxed for me?
- Have you considered how assets will be divided if beneficiaries live in different countries?
- Is your estate plan still aligned with where your children actually live today?

These discussions can feel uncomfortable, but they are acts of care, not conflict. They give parents the chance to make informed decisions. They give adult children context. And they reduce the risk that grief will be compounded by surprise, confusion, or unintended inequity.

THE REAL GOAL OF INTERNATIONAL ESTATE PLANNING

International estate planning is more about coordination than it is about control.

It's about understanding which laws apply to your life, where your choices are flexible, and where they are not. It's about using the right tools in the right countries and recognizing that what works at one stage of life may need to evolve as your family, assets, and residency change.

The goal is not to eliminate complexity, which is typically a futile endeavor in a cross-border life context. The goal is to make sure that complexity doesn't land on the people you love at the worst possible moment, when decisions are urgent, emotions are high, and options are limited.

CHAPTER FOURTEEN

HOW DO I KEEP MY ESTATE PLAN WORKING AS MY LIFE CHANGES ABROAD?

Key Question: When should I update my estate plan, and how do I make sure it stays aligned with my life across borders?

If international estate planning feels overwhelming, it's often because people approach it as a single decision instead of an ongoing process.

Most Americans are taught that estate planning is something you "finish." You meet with a lawyer, sign documents, put them in a drawer, and move on. That model works, barely, when your life stays in one place. A global life doesn't work that way.

When you live abroad, your legal and tax environment changes. Facts that were formerly assets in one country may become liabilities requiring extensive reworking in another. And sometimes, the laws themselves change. An estate plan that is perfectly reasonable today can become outdated, misaligned, or even harmful a few years later.

When done correctly, international estate planning is about creating a system that can evolve with your life and weather headwinds generated by legislative headwinds, whose downstream effects are sometimes intentional, sometimes not, but always felt by expats caught in the crosshairs.

ESTATE PLANNING IS A PROCESS, NOT A PRODUCT

The most effective international estate plans are built around review points; you don't need to revisit everything constantly. But you do need to know *when* a review is necessary.

Common triggers include the following:

- Moving to a new country
- Changing residency or citizenship status
- Marriage, divorce, or remarriage
- The birth or adoption of a child
- Buying or selling property abroad
- A significant inheritance or liquidity event
- A change in local inheritance or tax law

Any one of these can change the environment:

- Which laws apply
- Who is legally recognized
- How assets are classified
- What your heirs will actually receive

Ignoring those shifts doesn't freeze your plan in place. It allows it to drift.

THINK IN LAYERS, NOT DOCUMENTS

One of the most helpful mindset shifts for expats is to stop thinking in terms of *documents* and start thinking in terms of *layers*.

Your international estate plan typically includes the following:

- Family law (who counts as family)
- Property law (who owns what)
- Estate and inheritance tax law
- Asset location rules
- Treaty overlays (if applicable)
- Practical administration and reporting realities

No single document controls all of that. Here are a few ways to think about the function of different documents:

- A will expresses intent.
- A trust may control timing or protection.
- Beneficiary designations move assets automatically.
- Local law sets boundaries you cannot contract around.

Strong planning coordinates these layers instead of assuming one tool overrides the rest.

THE RIGHT PROFESSIONALS (AND WHY COORDINATION MATTERS)

International estate planning is one of the clearest examples of where *good intentions fail without coordination.*

Most problems don't come from bad advice. They occur when advice is sought in silos, and advisors aren't encouraged (or perhaps not proactive enough) to collaborate.

As someone with international estate planning considerations, you may need one or all the following:

- A US estate planning attorney
- A local estate or inheritance attorney
- A cross-border tax advisor
- A cross-border financial planner who understands how assets and beneficiaries interact and can ideally coordinate your advisors

When advisors work in silos, gaps form:

- A US trust that creates tax issues abroad
- A local will that unintentionally revokes a US plan
- Beneficiary designations that undermine both

Your cross-border financial planner should help quarterback the process, ensuring decisions are made with the full picture in mind.

THE EMOTIONAL SIDE OF MAINTENANCE

One reason estate planning gets deferred is emotional fatigue. These topics are heavy. They force you to confront uncertainty, mortality, and uncomfortable family dynamics. That's normal.

But delaying updates doesn't delay consequences. It simply shifts them to people you care about, often at moments when they're least equipped to deal with them.

Maintaining your plan is an act of care. Not control. Not pessimism. Care.

If your life crosses borders, your estate plan must do the same, and it must keep moving as you do.

INTERNATIONAL ESTATE PLANNING CHECKLIST

This checklist is a practical way to bring clarity to a complex, cross-border life. You don't need to solve everything at once. But you do need to know where you stand. Use this checklist as a starting point to identify gaps, priorities, and conversations worth having.

Family and Legal Recognition

- ☐ Confirm your marriage or partnership is legally recognized in your country of residence.
- ☐ Verify that prior divorces are formally recognized where you live now.

- ☐ Confirm how your country of residence defines "spouse," "child," and "heir."
- ☐ Review whether stepchildren or adopted children are recognized locally as legal heirs.
- ☐ If applicable, confirm recognition and rights for same-sex or nonmarital partnerships.

Ownership and Marital Property

- ☐ Identify the marital property regime that applies where you live.
- ☐ Confirm whether any default regime applies automatically.
- ☐ Review how assets acquired during marriage are classified (individual vs. joint).
- ☐ Evaluate whether a prenuptial or postnuptial agreement is recognized locally.
- ☐ Understand how property ownership affects children from prior relationships.

Estate Documents

- ☐ Inventory existing estate documents (wills, trusts, powers of attorney, healthcare directives).
- ☐ Confirm which country's law governs each document.
- ☐ Identify whether documents assume US only rules that may not apply abroad.
- ☐ Evaluate whether you need one will or coordinated wills in multiple countries.
- ☐ Ensure documents align with local probate, language, and formality requirements.

Trusts and Beneficiaries

- ☐ Review whether existing trusts are recognized where you live.
- ☐ Assess whether trust assets could be pulled back under forced heirship rules.
- ☐ Review all beneficiary designations on retirement accounts, insurance, and investments.
- ☐ Confirm beneficiary choices align with forced heirship, tax, and residency realities.
- ☐ Consider the tax impact on heirs who live outside the United States.

Tax and Treaty Considerations

- ☐ Identify whether an estate or gift tax treaty applies to your situation.
- ☐ Understand what the treaty does *and does not* protect against.
- ☐ Assess exposure to foreign inheritance tax for you or your heirs.
- ☐ Consider whether heirs living abroad could face tax on US-based inheritances.
- ☐ Review state-level estate or inheritance tax exposure, if applicable.

Incapacity and Guardianship

- ☐ Confirm whether US powers of attorney and healthcare directives are recognized locally.
- ☐ Establish local incapacity documents if required.
- ☐ Name temporary local guardians for minor children, if applicable.
- ☐ Confirm long-term guardians can step in across borders if needed.
- ☐ Communicate guardianship plans clearly with all parties involved.

Family Communication

- ☐ Inform key family members where documents are stored and who to contact.
- ☐ Discuss cross-border tax and inheritance implications with aging parents.
- ☐ Clarify intent where outcomes may differ between heirs due to tax or residency.
- ☐ Revisit conversations as family locations, laws, or assets change.

Ongoing Review

- ☐ Revisit your estate plan after major life changes (move, marriage, divorce, birth, death).
- ☐ Review plans when changing countries or residency status.
- ☐ Coordinate between US and local professionals rather than planning in silos.
- ☐ Treat estate planning as a living process, not a one-time task.

A Final Reminder

Trying to get every box checked off on this list in quick succession is a recipe for administrative burnout, personal and possibly interpersonal frustration, and long-term decisions made from a place of impatience rather than understanding. When reviewing this list, I recommend focusing on which boxes matter *for your life right now* so that international estate planning feels like a manageable project rather than an overwhelming one.

CHAPTER FIFTEEN

WHAT CHANGES WHEN I MARRY A NON-US PARTNER?

Key Question: How do taxes, asset ownership, and financial planning work when one spouse is a US citizen and the other is not?

Falling in love across borders is one of the most human reasons people end up living abroad. It's also one of the least discussed financial turning points in an expat's life.

When a US citizen marries a non-US resident and builds a life abroad, money stops being just personal. It becomes political, legal, and cross-border, often in ways neither partner anticipated. The rules that apply to you as an individual US expat don't simply "blend" with the system of your partner's country. They stack. And sometimes they collide.

This chapter breaks down how tax filing status changes, why asset structure becomes a powerful planning lever, where common mistakes arise, and where thoughtful coordination can actually create new financial opportunities. It's about removing the surprise factor. Understanding that reality early is what prevents most of the stress mixed-nationality couples face.

MARRIAGE ABROAD DOESN'T CHANGE YOUR US CITIZENSHIP (BUT IT CHANGES ALMOST EVERYTHING ELSE)

One of the most important things to understand upfront is this: marriage does not change the fact that US citizens and green card holders remain tied to the US tax system.

You are still a US taxpayer on your foreign income. Your non-US spouse is not, unless and until they become a US tax resident themselves. That asymmetry is the source of many downstream decisions.

At the federal level, when a US citizen marries a non-US spouse, the default filing options are limited. Joint filing is only available if the non-US spouse elects to be treated as a US taxpayer, which pulls their worldwide income and assets into the US system. For many couples, that election may create more problems than it solves (https://www.irs.gov/individuals/international-taxpayers/nonresident-spouse).

As a result, many mixed-nationality couples initially file married filing separately (MFS). This is often and accurately described as the most punitive filing status in the US tax code, and not because it's rare or exotic, but because it was never designed for globally mobile families.

What makes MFS especially problematic is its low filing threshold. For taxpayers filing MFS, the US federal income tax filing requirement is triggered at just $5 of gross income. This threshold has not been inflation-adjusted, unlike nearly every other filing status in the tax code.

In practical terms, this means that a US citizen filing MFS will almost always be required to file a US tax return, even if they have no wages at all. A small amount of bank interest, a modest dividend, or minimal investment income is usually enough to trigger a filing obligation. For expats, this is especially common, as foreign bank accounts often generate small amounts of taxable interest by default.

Once required to file, MFS significantly limits access to common tax benefits. Many deductions and credits are reduced or eliminated entirely, including education credits, certain retirement contributions, and favorable phase-outs that apply under other filing statuses. Marginal tax rates can be higher, and the ability to offset income with exclusions or credits can be less flexible.

For US expats married to non-US spouses, MFS is often the default, not because it's ideal, but because the alternatives carry their own trade-offs. Electing to file jointly can fully subject a non-US spouse to US tax rules, subjecting their global income and assets to ongoing US reporting requirements. Despite these drawbacks, many couples choose MFS as the lesser of two complexities, at least initially.

Understanding how easily the filing requirement is triggered—and how limited the benefits become once you're there—is essential to planning intentionally rather than reacting under pressure. This is also why filing strategy often evolves over time, particularly once children, changes in income, or long-term residency decisions enter the picture.

ASSET SEPARATION: STRATEGY, NOT FEAR

One of the most common pieces of advice US expats married to non-US partners hear is some version of *just keep everything in your non-US spouse's name.*

Sometimes that advice is helpful. Sometimes it's incomplete. And sometimes it creates risks that are far more serious than the ones it was meant to solve.

The instinct behind this guidance is easy to understand. US tax and reporting rules FBAR, FATCA, and Form 8938 can make joint accounts and foreign investments feel intimidating, especially when the non-US spouse has no connection to the American tax system. Keeping certain assets unattached to the US person's name can, in the right circumstances, reduce reporting complexity and limit how much of the household is pulled into US compliance.

But strategic planning is not the same thing as erasing the US spouse from the balance sheet.

In real life, asset separation is rarely as clean as it sounds. Joint accounts may still trigger FBAR or FATCA reporting if the US spouse has signature authority or access, even without ownership. Completely separating assets can leave the US spouse financially vulnerable in the event of divorce, death, or incapacity. And in many countries, marital property laws apply regardless of whose name appears on an account, meaning informal assumptions about ownership may not hold up when it matters most.

This is why asset separation should be approached as a planning strategy, not a fear response.

For many mixed-nationality couples, the most effective approach isn't "everything joint" or "everything separate," but a thoughtful combination of both:

- Using a mix of separate and joint accounts, based on purpose rather than anxiety
- Clearly documenting ownership, especially for large assets or inherited funds
- Understanding when shared use crosses into shared ownership under local law
- Reviewing how marital property regimes affect assets regardless of title

One of the most powerful and often misunderstood tools in this conversation is interspousal gifting.

Interspousal Gifting: Powerful, but Not Unlimited

In the United States, gifts between spouses are typically unlimited. But that rule changes when one spouse is not a US citizen.

Gifts from a US citizen to a non-US spouse are subject to an annual marital gift exclusion, which is generous but capped and adjusted for inflation each year (for example, $194,000 in 2026). Gifts above that amount begin to eat into the US spouse's lifetime gift and estate exemption and must be reported.

Used intentionally, this threshold can be an excellent planning opportunity. Couples may decide, for example:

- That the non-US spouse holds certain investment assets in a country with favorable tax treatment, keeping those assets completely outside the US reporting.
- That assets are shifted gradually over time rather than all at once

But this is where nuance matters.

Once a gift is complete, that asset is no longer the US spouse's property. That can be beneficial from a US tax perspective, but it also has real legal consequences. In the event of divorce, gifted assets may not be considered marital property. In the event of death, those assets may be subject to inheritance or estate tax in the spouse's country of residence. And in some jurisdictions, gifting itself can trigger local tax or reporting obligations.

So, the critical question becomes: Is this a strategic allocation of family assets, or an irreversible transfer of ownership? The answer depends on where you live, where the assets are located, how local marital property laws apply, and what you are trying to protect against.

The goal of asset separation is not to make the US spouse "disappear" from the financial picture. That approach often backfires.

The real goal is to design a system that accomplishes the following:

- Reduces unnecessary tax and reporting friction
- Protects both spouses financially
- Holds up in divorce, death, or incapacity
- Aligns with local marital property law
- Reflects how the family actually lives and earns
- Optimize tax and financial planning opportunities from a US and foreign perspective

For US citizens married to non-US spouses, asset structure is one of the most meaningful planning levers available, but only when it's done with full awareness of the trade-offs. US citizens living abroad and married to non-US persons actually have more planning tools available to them than US persons married to other US persons, so while this does add some additional planning considerations, it does also add more planning opportunities.

This is exactly the kind of decision that benefits from professional guidance. The rules are nuanced, highly country-specific, and deeply interconnected with tax, estate, and family law. Getting it right rarely requires fear. It requires clarity.

> **Expert Insight:** *Cultures are different. We grow up in different contexts, with different ways of communicating, showing love, disagreeing, and building trust. What may feel obvious or "normal" in one culture doesn't always translate in another.*
>
> *That's why open, intentional communication becomes essential in multicultural relationships.*
>
> *To keep your relationship strong across borders, start with three things: values, boundaries, and fears.*
>
> ***Values** help steer the direction of your life together. Try this exercise: each partner writes down two core values, then talk through what they actually mean.*
>
> *For example, both of you might say "financial security." But to one person, that could mean owning property. To the other, it might mean flexibility and having the freedom to travel. The word is the same, but the meaning is different. The clarity comes from the conversation.*
>
> ***Boundaries** define what you need to feel grounded and supported. In a cross-border life, these can shape major decisions. It might sound like:*
>
> - *"I don't want to live too far from my family."*
> - *"I don't want to move somewhere I need to learn another language."*
> - *"I need more structure around time with extended family."*
>
> *When boundaries are clear, decisions become easier to navigate together.*

(Continued)

(Continued)

> ***Fears*** *are often the most powerful, and the most overlooked. They show where support is needed most.*
>
> *You might fear living in your partner's country, losing connection to your culture, or raising children far from your support system. When those fears are shared openly, they create opportunities for deeper understanding and partnership.*
>
> *This isn't a one-time conversation. It's something to revisit regularly—every few months or during major life transitions like moving countries, career changes, or having children.*
>
> *Strong cross-border relationships aren't built on perfect alignment. They're built on clarity, communication, and a shared commitment to navigating differences together.*
>
> *—Angela Vitiello, MBA, MS Ed, CMT-P, Expat Parenting Collective*

When Things Don't Go According to Plan

No one enters a marriage expecting it to end. But for couples building a life across borders, separation or divorce carries layers of complexity that domestic couples rarely must confront.

When a US citizen and a non-US person divorce while living abroad, the consequences extend well beyond emotional and financial stress. Immigration status, residency rights, asset division, and even the ability to remain in the country can all be affected, sometimes immediately.

One of the most common and underestimated issues is residency. In many countries, a non-citizen spouse's right to live and work locally may be tied directly to the marriage. If that marriage ends, residency privileges may end with it. Some countries offer pathways to retain residence after divorce, such as long-term residence permits, employment-based visas, or hardship provisions. Others do not. The result is that one spouse may be forced to make rapid decisions about employment, housing, or relocation at the same time they are navigating a legal separation.

Asset division can be equally complicated. Divorce does not follow a universal rulebook. Depending on the country, the following might apply:

- Marital property may be split under community property, equitable distribution, or contractual regimes.
- Assets may be divided based on local law, regardless of how they are titled or what a US agreement assumes.
- Property located in different countries may be governed by different legal systems at the same time.

What feels "fair" may not align with how another country allocates assets or recognizes ownership. In some cases, a divorce judgment issued in one country must be formally recognized in another before it has any legal effect, which can delay settlements or create conflicting obligations.

Tax consequences can also diverge sharply. The treatment of alimony, lump-sum settlements, and asset transfers varies widely by jurisdiction. A division that is tax-neutral in one country may trigger taxable events in another. Without coordinated planning, divorcing couples can unintentionally create tax liabilities that neither party anticipated.

This is not a reason to assume the worst. It *is* a reason to acknowledge that cross-border marriages operate inside multiple systems at once, and those systems don't automatically harmonize when a relationship changes.

For international couples, prenuptial agreements, postnuptial agreements, and marital agreements are not about pessimism. They are about clarity. They can do the following:

- Define how assets will be treated across jurisdictions
- Address default marital property regimes before they apply automatically
- Anticipate residency or immigration consequences
- Reduce uncertainty if the relationship no longer follows its original path

Timing matters. Agreements and planning done early before relocation, marriage, or major asset accumulation offer far more flexibility than planning done under pressure.

In cross-border lives, planning for *change* is part of planning well. The goal isn't to predict failure. It's to avoid being trapped by legal and financial systems you didn't realize you were subject to until it was too late.

CHAPTER SIXTEEN

WHAT CHANGES WHEN YOU HAVE CHILDREN ABROAD?

Key Question: How do children reshape your taxes, citizenship, and long-term planning as a US expat family?

Few events anchor an international life as powerfully as the birth of a child. Before children, many mixed-nationality couples experience their life abroad as flexible. Moves feel reversible. Systems feel negotiable. Residency, taxes, and even long-term plans often remain intentionally vague. When children enter the picture, that flexibility narrows. Decisions start to carry longer shadows, and financial, legal, and tax systems begin to matter in ways they didn't before.

For US citizens married to non-US partners, parenthood is often the moment when US tax rules stop feeling theoretical and start shaping real outcomes. One of the first visible shifts happens at the tax level.

Expert Insight: *Children will change everything. Whether it's the loss of spontaneous travel or the deep emotional shift that comes with parenthood, life becomes more anchored, and both partners feel it.*

For cross-border couples, one of the most important steps is having intentional conversations about parenting early. Even couples from the same culture don't parent the same way. When you come from different cultural backgrounds, those differences can be even more pronounced.

Start by understanding each other's foundation: What did parenting look like growing up? Share the good, the bad, and the difficult. In moments of stress, these early experiences often become your default.

Then look forward: How do you want to show up as a parent? What does that actually look like day to day? These conversations help clarify expectations and give your partner insight into how to support you.

If something feels vague, ask: What does that mean to you? What does that look like in practice?

From there, shift into the practical realities of raising children abroad: How will you divide responsibilities? How will you balance careers and parenting? How will you navigate language, culture, and traditions in a country that may not be home for either of you?

For example, in a multilingual household, how will language be spoken and reinforced? If both partners value their careers, how will decisions be made when those priorities conflict with time at home?

These questions don't go away if they're avoided. They tend to resurface in moments of stress, often with more intensity. Addressing them early creates alignment instead of friction.

> *These conversations require vulnerability. But they also create something stronger: clarity, partnership, and a shared foundation for raising a family across borders with intention.*
>
> *—Angela Vitiello MBA, MS Ed, CMT-P, Expat Parenting Collective*

HEAD OF HOUSEHOLD: A FILING STATUS THAT REFLECTS REALITY

When children are born, many US expats married to non-US citizens eventually move away from Married Filing Separately (MFS) and into Head of Household (HOH) status.

While still imperfect, HOH is often far more favorable than MFS. Importantly, it reflects a common reality for expat families: the US citizen is often carrying the full weight of US tax compliance for a household that otherwise doesn't exist inside the US system at all.

HOH is frequently misunderstood, especially by couples who assume that being legally married automatically disqualifies them. Under US tax law, that's not always true.

A married person may file as HOH if they fall under "married but considered unmarried" for tax purposes at the end of the year. For US expats married to non-US spouses living abroad, this status is often available when several conditions are met:

- First, the US citizen must not elect to file jointly with the non-US spouse. Filing jointly would pull the spouse's worldwide income and assets into the US tax system, something many families intentionally avoid.

- Second, the US citizen must have a qualifying child under US tax rules. In practice, most children born to US citizens abroad qualify, often because they are US citizens at birth, even if that citizenship has not yet been formally documented.
- Third, the US citizen must pay more than half the cost of maintaining the household. For expat families, this typically includes rent, housing costs, food, healthcare, education, childcare, and general living expenses. Finally, the non-US spouse must be considered a nonresident alien for the entire tax year and must not live in the United States at any point during the last six months of the year. A spouse who lives abroad full-time generally satisfies this requirement.

When these conditions are met, the IRS allows the US citizen spouse to file as HOH, despite being legally married.

Why HOH Filing Status Matters So Much

HOH status can materially improve a family's tax position. It provides a higher standard deduction, more favorable tax brackets, and access to credits that are limited or unavailable under MFS. It also aligns more naturally with Child Tax Credit rules.

For many US expat parents, HOH is the first filing status that feels even remotely aligned with lived reality. It acknowledges that the US citizen is supporting dependents, complying with US tax law, and absorbing financial responsibility while the family's actual life unfolds somewhere else.

That said, HOH is not automatic, and it is not permanent. If a non-US spouse later moves to the United States, obtains a green card, or if the couple elects to file jointly, HOH may disappear. If a child no longer qualifies as a dependent, the status can also end. And because HOH depends heavily on facts and circumstances, documentation matters.

This is why tax professionals working with expat families ask questions that can feel unusually detailed: where each family member lived, who paid which expenses, how dependency rules are met, and whether any joint elections were made.

YOUR CHILDREN ARE PROBABLY US CITIZENS, WHETHER YOU REGISTERED THEM OR NOT

This is one of the most emotionally charged and least understood realities for mixed-nationality families.

In many cases, children born abroad to a US citizen parent are US citizens at birth, even if they were born outside the United States, have never lived there, and do not yet have a US passport or Social Security number. Citizenship is conferred by law, not by paperwork. Failing to register it doesn't erase it; it simply delays formal recognition.

That distinction feels abstract when children are young. It becomes very real later when those children apply to university, open bank or investment accounts, move countries, inherit assets, or attempt to confirm, or renounce, citizenship as adults.

From a financial planning perspective, this matters deeply. US citizenship comes with lifelong tax and reporting obligations unless it is formally renounced. For some families, that connection is a benefit. For others, it's a burden they wish they had understood earlier.

Children don't just expand your family. They anchor your legal, tax, and financial footprint in ways that are difficult to unwind later. Recognizing that early doesn't force a single "right" decision, but it does give families the ability to choose intentionally rather than reactively.

> **Expert Insight:** *Don't forget to take "vacations" when visiting the United States. It's so easy to fall into the trap of running around and only visiting family and friends when returning to the United States. While reconnecting with our loved ones in person is so important, don't forget to let yourself (and your spouse/kids if traveling with you) enjoy what the United States has to offer. Make sure to schedule some real vacation time in between your personal visits.*
>
> *—Kaitlin Krozel, CPA, Krozel Capital*

FAMILY ESTATE PLANNING DOESN'T ALWAYS TRAVEL WELL

When children are born, estate planning changes everywhere. But outside the United States, it can change in ways that directly limit your freedom to decide who inherits what.

Many Americans assume that having a will means they control how their estate is distributed. In the United States, that assumption is largely correct. In many other countries, it is not.

A significant number of countries operate under forced heirship rules. These laws require that a portion of your estate pass to legally protected heirs, most commonly children, regardless of what your will says.

Once children exist, your ability to freely distribute assets may be permanently constrained.

Forced heirship regimes vary by country, but they often work as follows:

- Mandate minimum inheritance shares for children
- Limit how much can pass to a spouse
- Override beneficiary designations and trusts
- Apply to assets located locally, and sometimes worldwide
- Apply regardless of citizenship, based on residence or domicile

For US citizens married to non-US spouses, this can complicate planning dramatically. Children may have guaranteed inheritance rights under local law, while a spouse's rights depend on marital property regimes, citizenship, or residency status. In blended families, the impact can be even more pronounced, with children from prior relationships receiving statutory shares that conflict with US-based intentions.

What makes forced heirship especially difficult for expats is that it often applies automatically, without any affirmative choice. You don't "opt in" to these rules. You discover them only when you try to plan around them, or worse, when your family is already grieving.

Some countries allow limited planning around forced heirship through elections, marital agreements, or EU succession regulations. Others do not. And while tax treaties may coordinate estate taxation, they do not override inheritance law.

Once children exist, estate planning abroad is no longer just about taxes or documents. It's about understanding which legal system gets to decide what your children are entitled to, and whether your current plan actually works where you live.

This is why families with children should revisit estate planning after relocation, not just after marriage or asset accumulation. The arrival of a child often changes the legal outcome more than any other life event. We will discuss this in more detail in the coming chapters on estate planning.

DIVORCE WITH CHILDREN ABROAD

No one wants to imagine their marriage ending. But when children are involved in a cross-border life, the consequences of divorce extend far beyond finances.

One of the most difficult realities for expat parents to confront is this: having children in a country can effectively anchor you there, regardless of whether you still want to be there or not.

In many situations, once children are habitually resident in a country, one parent cannot unilaterally leave with them, even if both parents originally agreed the move was "temporary"; even if the marriage is deteriorating; even if one parent desperately wants to return home.

International custody disputes are governed in part by the Hague Convention on the Civil Aspects of International Child Abduction, a treaty designed to prevent one parent from wrongfully removing or retaining a child across borders. While the treaty's intent is protective, its effect can feel harsh when a relationship breaks down.

The following apply under the Hague Convention:

- A child's habitual residence becomes the key legal concept.
- Verbal agreements about trial moves often carry little weight.
- Courts prioritize returning a child to their country of habitual residence.
- Parents who remove children without consent may be ordered to return them.

What many expat families don't realize is how quickly "habitual residence" can be established. Months, not years, can be enough. Once established, a parent may be legally prevented from relocating with their children without the other parent's consent or a court order.

This is why trial moves, sabbaticals, or "let's see how it goes" relocations should be documented, not just discussed. Written agreements, clear timelines, and legal advice before relocation matter far more than people expect.

If a relationship is deteriorating and children are involved, timing becomes critical. Announcing intentions before understanding your legal position can permanently limit your options. Residency rules, custody law, and international treaties interact quickly once formal proceedings begin. This is not a reason to live in fear. But it is a reason to be informed.

For international families, working with professionals who understand cross-border family law is essential as domestic divorce advice on its own is often insufficient. The legal system that governs your marriage, your residency, and your children may not be the same, and the order in which issues are addressed can change outcomes dramatically. Planning does not assume failure. It acknowledges complexity.

Money and marriage abroad require a mindset shift. This is not about choosing between love and logic. It's about respecting that cross-border lives are structurally more complex, and complexity rewards early, thoughtful planning.

The healthiest international couples don't aim to "hide" from systems. They learn how the systems work, decide where alignment matters most, and make deliberate choices that protect both partners and their children over time.

This book aims to continue building on this foundation, looking at how these family dynamics intersect with estate planning, long-term investing, and life transitions. But everything starts here: understanding that when you marry across borders, money becomes a shared language spoken in more than one legal system. Clarity doesn't eliminate risk. It gives you agency.

Expert Insight: *I've worked with many clients who only seek tax advice after major decisions have already been finalized, divorce agreements, business structures, or financial settlements negotiated entirely without considering the US tax implications alongside the local country rules.*

The common thread is this: What saved time upfront often ended up costing significantly more in taxes, compliance issues, or limited options later.

One example stands out. A US client went through a divorce abroad and, together with local counsel, agreed to a settlement requiring him to pay 40% of his salary as alimony. What wasn't considered was how that agreement would be treated under US tax law.

After 2017, alimony is no longer deductible for US tax purposes.

While the country of residence allowed a deduction, the mismatch between systems meant the client received limited tax relief locally but was still taxed on his full income in the United States. The result was devastating: after meeting his obligations, there was very little left.

A short conversation during the negotiation phase could have completely changed the outcome. Once agreements are signed, options become limited, and renegotiation is rarely simple or even possible.

This applies far beyond divorce.

Before entering into any major financial decision across borders, whether it's structuring a business, setting up a trust, or negotiating a settlement, it is critical to understand both sides of the system: US tax rules and the rules of your country of residence.

Cross-border planning is not something to retrofit after the fact. It needs to be part of the decision-making process from the beginning.

—Chad Hatalla, EA, CFP®, Hatalla Tax

PART V

THE OPTION TO RETURN

CHAPTER SEVENTEEN

WHAT HAPPENS IF I DECIDE TO MOVE BACK TO THE UNITED STATES?

Key Question: How do you return to the United States without creating unnecessary tax, financial, and logistical friction?

You may be wondering why a chapter about moving back to the United States belongs in a book about moving abroad. The answer is simple: the strongest international moves are made with the exit plan in mind from day one.

You might be moving abroad for a defined chapter, work, education, or a few years of adventure. Or you might be one of the many Americans who move overseas and eventually realize they love traveling internationally but prefer building their long-term life in the United States. For others, the plan evolves slowly and unexpectedly.

Some people return sooner than expected because of family needs, health concerns, career shifts, or political changes. Others stay abroad for decades and return later in life. And many end up living a hybrid life, splitting time between the United States and another country as priorities shift.

The goal of this chapter isn't to assume you'll move back. It's to make sure that if you ever choose to, you can do so on your terms, financially prepared, informed, and without unnecessary friction.

SECTION 1: THE TAX SIDE OF COMING HOME (WHERE TIMING MATTERS)

The biggest financial mistakes around repatriation usually aren't about *what* you do. They're about *when* you do it. Taxes are one of the few areas where timing can quietly turn a good decision into an expensive one.

Departing or returning to the United States doesn't flip a simple switch from "expat taxes" to "normal taxes." Instead, the transition year often layers multiple tax systems on top of one another. Understanding how those layers interact is what separates a smooth return from an expensive one.

> **Expert Insights:** *Many US expats become used to the automatic June 15th filing deadline while living abroad. But that extension doesn't always apply in the year you return.*
>
> *The key detail: your filing deadline is based on where you live at the time the return is due, not where you lived during the prior tax year.*
>
> *For example, Joe lived in Spain for five years and moved back to the United States on February 15. He assumes that because he spent the entire prior tax year abroad, his return is due June 15. That's not correct.*

> *Because Joe is living in the United States when the filing deadline arrives, his tax return is due April 15.*
>
> *—Kaitlin Krozel, CPA, Krozel Capital*

US Tax Residency Never Fully Turns Off

If you are a **US citizen** or a **US green card holder**, you are always considered a **US tax resident at the federal level**, regardless of where you live. Moving abroad does not change that status, and returning to the United States doesn't restore it because it was never gone.

What *does* change while you live abroad is how your foreign income is taxed.

As discussed in Chapter 1, Americans living overseas may be able to reduce or eliminate double taxation by using tools like the Foreign Earned Income Exclusion (FEIE) and the Foreign Tax Credit (FTC). These provisions don't change your residency; they change how income earned abroad is treated.

When you return to the United States, those tools don't disappear overnight, but how and when you use them becomes especially important.

Departure and Return Years: Where Complexity Peaks

The years you move are often the most complex tax year of your entire expat journey. That's because it usually includes the following:

- Income earned abroad that may still qualify for FEIE or FTC
- Income earned in the United States under full domestic tax rules

- A change (or re-establishment) of **state tax residency**, which follows its own rules

This mix is where timing matters most.

FEIE for Your Final Expat Months

You can still claim the FEIE for income earned while you were abroad, even in the year you return.

Key points to understand:

- The FEIE is prorated based on the number of qualifying days you spent abroad.
- The full 2025 exclusion is $132,900 (adjusted for inflation annually), but return-year exclusions are reduced proportionally.
- You must still meet either the Physical Presence Test or Bona Fide Residence Test for the foreign portion of the year.

This allows many returning expats to exclude a meaningful amount of foreign income, even though they spend part of the year back in the United States.

Foreign Tax Credit Optimization in the Return Year

The Foreign Tax Credit often becomes even more valuable during a return year.

FTC rules allow you to

- claim credits for foreign income taxes paid while abroad,
- carry back credits one year, and
- carry forward unused credits for up to 10 years.

In many cases, properly applied foreign tax credits can fully offset US tax on foreign income earned before your return.

This is why selling assets, receiving bonuses, or finalizing compensation before or after your move date can materially change your tax outcome.

State Taxes: The Not So Silent Complication

Federal tax rules are only half the story when you move back to the United States.

State taxes are where many returning expats are caught off guard.

Unlike federal taxes, state tax residency is not uniform. It often hinges on a mix of intent, physical presence, and personal ties, and some states are far more aggressive than others about claiming you as a resident, even while you're living abroad or splitting time.

Certain states are known for taking a hard line on residency, especially if you maintain strong ties. States like California, New York, New Jersey, Massachusetts, and Virginia are frequently cited as more aggressive in residency audits.

A state may continue to treat you as a resident if you maintain the following indicators:

- An available residence (owned or leased)
- Regular or predictable travel back to the state
- Immediate family members living there
- A state driver's license or ID
- Voter registration
- Bank accounts, doctors, or professional licenses tied to the state

Moving abroad doesn't automatically end state residency. And returning, even briefly, can restart the clock faster than people expect.

This is why your accountant will ask questions that feel oddly specific:

- How many days did you spend in each state?
- Where were you physically working?
- When did you re-establish a permanent home?
- When did you change licenses, voter registration, or mailing addresses?

These details matter. Especially now.

Remote Work Changed the Rules (and the Enforcement)

Post-COVID, states have become far more aggressive about **remote workers** and **split-location lifestyles**. Working "temporarily" from a state, even for a few weeks, can create tax exposure if the state views that work as sourced locally.

For returning expats who plan to

- split time between states,
- ease back into US life gradually, or
- work remotely before settling permanently
  state tax rules need to be reviewed *before* you land.

Travel logs, calendars, and documentation of where you worked, not just where you slept, can make or break a state tax position.

Not All States Follow Federal Expat Rules

Another common misconception: states are not required to follow federal tax exclusions.

Most notably, many states do not recognize the FEIE. Even if your foreign income is excluded at the federal level, it may still be fully taxable at the state level.

States that have historically not conformed to the FEIE include (but are not limited to):

- California
- New Jersey
- Pennsylvania
- Massachusetts

This means you could

- owe **zero federal tax** on foreign income and
- still owe **state tax** on that same income.

This disconnect is one of the most expensive surprises for expats who return to, or never fully sever ties with, high-tax states.

The Big Takeaway on State Taxes

State tax planning should happen **before you return**, not after you unpack:

- The date you establish (or re-establish) residency matters.
- The state you return to matters.
- The ties you maintain, even unintentionally, matter.

And once a state claims you as a resident, unwinding that position can be time-consuming, expensive, and stressful.

Example Expat

While US citizens remain federal tax residents all year, it's still helpful to think of the return year in two functional phases:

- **Foreign period:** Time spent abroad, where FEIE and/or FTC may apply

- **US period:** Time spent back in the United States, with full access to domestic tax benefits

Example: Timing Done Right

Jane returned to New York City on July 1, 2025, after working in Mexico.

- She spent half the year abroad and qualifies for FEIE for that period.
- She can exclude up to **$65,000** of her Mexican income (50% of the $66,450 annual FEIE limit).
- Once back in the United States, she regains full access to domestic tax benefits, including standard deductions and retirement contributions.

However, Jane's planning doesn't stop at the federal level.

By re-establishing residency in New York City (NYC), she also becomes subject to New York State and NYC income taxes for the portion of the year she is considered a resident. And here's where many returning expats are caught off guard.

Even though New York/NYC may only tax Jane on the income she earns *after* returning, the state and city may still use her entire annual income to determine the marginal tax rate applied to that New York–sourced income.

In practice, this means:

- Her excluded foreign income may still push her into a higher New York and NYC tax bracket.
- The income she earns after returning can be taxed at a higher rate than expected.
- State and city taxes can materially change the outcome, even when federal planning is done well.

Jane still benefits significantly from careful timing and use of the FEIE, but her total tax picture only makes sense once state and local rules are layered in.

This is why repatriation planning can't focus on federal taxes alone. The interaction between foreign income, federal exclusions or credits, and state residency rules is where the real complexity and opportunity lie. These are the years we highly recommend seeking professional support for your tax planning and preparation.

SECTION 2: MOVING MONEY BACK TO THE UNITED STATES (IT'S NOT JUST A WIRE TRANSFER)

On paper, repatriating assets looks simple: transfer the money back to the United States. In practice, it's rarely that clean.

When you move home, you're not just moving cash. You're unwinding years of financial decisions made inside a different legal, tax, and regulatory system. Each account has its own rules, and many of them don't line up neatly with the US system.

Foreign Accounts Don't Always Translate Well

Foreign banks and investment platforms are built for residents, not for people who are leaving.

As you prepare to move money back, you may encounter the following:

- Restrictions on transfers to US institutions
- Compliance reviews or delays for large transactions
- Foreign account closures once you're no longer a local resident

At the same time, US banks and brokerages are required to scrutinize incoming foreign funds. It's common for them to do the following:

- Request source-of-funds documentation
- Ask for copies of foreign account statements or contracts
- Place temporary holds on large transfers while compliance reviews are completed

Foreign Retirement Accounts: Often Cash-out, Not Transfer

One of the biggest surprises for returning expats is what happens to foreign retirement or pension accounts.

Unlike US retirement accounts, foreign pensions cannot be transferred into US-style accounts like IRAs or 401(k)s. There is no universal "roll-over" mechanism across borders.

In many cases, your options are limited:

- Leave the account in place under local rules, potentially in cash.
- Take distributions according to the foreign system's schedule at retirement.
- Cash out the account.

Each option comes with trade-offs:

Cashing out a foreign retirement account may trigger local taxes, US taxes, or both, depending on the country, the type of plan, and whether a tax treaty applies.

Leaving funds abroad, however, can create a different set of risks that are quieter and sometimes more costly over time. From a US tax perspective, not all foreign retirement accounts are clearly recognized as "retirement" accounts at all. If the IRS does not view the account as tax-deferred under US rules or treaty protection, the investments inside it may be treated like regular foreign investment accounts. That can lead to several unintended consequences.

First, ongoing US reporting requirements may continue indefinitely. Many foreign retirement accounts trigger FBAR and FATCA reporting every year, even after you return to the United States. Compliance doesn't end just because you no longer live abroad.

Second, investment growth may be taxed annually by the United States, even if the foreign country does not tax it until withdrawal. This can destroy the long-term tax efficiency of the account from a US perspective.

Third and often most damaging, foreign retirement accounts that hold non-US mutual funds or pooled investments can fall under the **Passive Foreign Investment Company (PFIC)** regime. PFIC rules impose punitive tax treatment, complex annual reporting, and unfavorable timing rules on gains and distributions. In some cases, the compliance cost alone exceeds the value of the account.

Finally, many foreign financial institutions restrict what US persons are allowed to hold once flagged under FATCA. After you return to the United States, you may find that

- your investment options are frozen,
- new investments are limited to cash or low-yield products, or
- the institution pressures you to close the account altogether.

Foreign retirement accounts often require **intentional exit planning**, not passive neglect. In some cases, taking distributions before returning, restructuring investments while still resident abroad, or coordinating withdrawals across tax years can dramatically reduce long-term friction and tax exposure.

Annual distributions can continue to create tax complexity even after you return to the United States, especially if investments make ongoing, annual distributions. Many countries apply mandatory tax withholding at the source, which doesn't automatically stop when you leave, meaning you may still need to file foreign tax returns to recover or credit that tax. In the United States, those same distributions may be taxed differently, depending on the account type and whether a tax treaty applies, creating timing mismatches or unused foreign tax credits. The result is that a single foreign income stream can lock you into years of cross-border tax reporting unless it's planned carefully.

This is especially important for expats returning after long careers overseas. What feels like "retirement savings" in a foreign system may function very differently once you're back under US tax rules. The mistake to avoid is assuming you can simply move or consolidate everything once you return. In many cases, decisions around foreign pensions need to be made before you leave, while you still have access to favorable local treatment or more flexible withdrawal options.

Currency Risk Returns, in Reverse

When you move back to the United States, currency risk doesn't disappear. It flips direction.

Converting foreign savings into dollars exposes you to several risks:

- Exchange-rate timing risk
- Market volatility if investments must be sold before transfer
- Emotional pressure to "pick the right moment"

Trying to perfectly time currency moves often backfires. Exchange rates are unpredictable, and waiting for the "ideal" rate can delay access to funds you actually need.

For most people, a phased approach works better:

- Move money gradually rather than all at once
- Maintain short-term reserves in both currencies during the transition
- Prioritize liquidity and cash flow over exchange-rate perfection

The goal isn't to optimize the exchange rate. It's to make sure you can pay rent, buy a car, and cover daily expenses without stress while your finances resettle.

SECTION 3: THE COST OF REVERSE CULTURE SHOCK

Most expats expect some degree of reverse culture shock when they return to the United States. What catches many off guard is how intense that shock can be financially.

After years abroad, many returning Americans are surprised to discover that the baseline cost of living in the United States is significantly higher than they remembered. Housing costs often feel steep, especially in major metro areas. Childcare expenses can be jarring compared to public or subsidized options overseas. Healthcare once again becomes tightly tied to employment, bringing higher premiums, deductibles, and out-of-pocket costs back into the picture. Transportation frequently assumes car ownership, reintroducing insurance, maintenance, and fuel as nonnegotiable monthly expenses.

At the same time, reverse culture shock shows up in more subtle ways through day-to-day spending. Many returnees find themselves paying for convenience in ways they didn't need abroad: more delivery, more driving, more paid help, and more "just make this easier" choices. These decisions aren't careless; they're a natural response to adjusting to a faster pace, different expectations, and systems that suddenly feel more complex or less forgiving than before.

One of the most common mistakes is assuming that a pre-expat US budget still applies. In reality, coming home usually involves a transition period with overlapping costs: temporary housing, gaps or overlaps in insurance, setup expenses for utilities, vehicles, and childcare, and higher short-term spending while routines and stability are rebuilt.

A realistic re-entry plan treats the first year back as transitional, not representative. Just like your first year abroad, your first year home is rarely a true picture of long-term costs. The most successful returnees don't try to recreate their old financial life immediately. They build in room for recalibration, financially and emotionally, and give themselves permission to adjust without judgment.

That flexibility is often what leads to better long-term decisions, lower stress, and a smoother transition back into life in the United States.

Repatriation Readiness Checklist

Use this checklist if a return to the United States is possible in the next one to three years

Tax Planning and Timing

- ☐ Confirm your expected return window (even a rough estimate helps with planning).
- ☐ Review how the FEIE and FTC apply in a return year.
- ☐ Identify which foreign income, bonuses, or asset sales may be better timed before or after your return.
- ☐ Understand whether your return year will include foreign income and US income in the same tax year.
- ☐ Plan for US state tax residency, including the following:
    - Which state you may return to
    - How aggressively that state enforces residency
    - What ties (housing, licenses, voting, family) could trigger residency sooner than expected

State Tax and Residency Awareness

- ☐ Confirm whether your state recognizes or disallows the FEIE.
- ☐ Track days worked and days present in each state if you're splitting time.

- ☐ Maintain travel logs and work location records, especially if working remotely.
- ☐ Avoid re-establishing strong state ties prematurely if you want to delay residency.

Foreign Accounts and Asset Strategy

- ☐ Review all foreign bank, investment, and retirement accounts for the following:
  - Ongoing FBAR and FATCA reporting requirements
  - US tax treatment of income and growth
- ☐ Identify foreign retirement or pension accounts where the following might apply:
  - Cannot be rolled into US accounts
  - May trigger PFIC exposure
  - May restrict investment options once you're a nonresident and US person
- ☐ Decide whether distributions, restructuring, or cash-outs should occur before returning.
- ☐ Plan for annual distributions that may require ongoing foreign tax filings or FTC claims.

Currency and Cash Flow Planning

- ☐ Decide how much local currency cash to keep during the transition.
- ☐ Avoid converting all funds at once if you have significant assets ($350k+); consider a phased transfer strategy.
- ☐ Prioritize liquidity over exchange-rate optimization during re-entry to ensure appropriate cash reserves and reduce stress.
- ☐ Anticipate short-term US setup costs (housing, car, insurance) when planning transfers.

US Financial Re-entry

- ☐ Keep at least one US bank account active while abroad if possible.
- ☐ Maintain or reopen a US credit card to preserve credit history.
- ☐ Prepare for credit reactivation, especially for housing or car financing.
- ☐ Review timing for employer benefits, including healthcare and retirement plans.

Cost-of-living Reset

- ☐ Build a transition budget for your first year back.
- ☐ Plan for overlapping costs:
  - Temporary housing
  - Insurance gaps or overlaps
  - Childcare or school setup
  - Transportation
- ☐ Expect higher baseline costs and allow for financial and emotional adjustment.
- ☐ Treat year one as transitional, not a benchmark for long-term spending.

Professional Support

- ☐ Engage a cross-border tax or financial planning professional before your return, not after.
- ☐ Coordinate federal and state tax planning together.
- ☐ Review foreign pensions, investments, and reporting obligations with US tax treatment in mind.

CHAPTER EIGHTEEN

EPILOGUE

When I first dreamed about living abroad, I thought I was optimizing for adventure. Long before Harry Potter made boarding schools in the United Kingdom feel romantic and attainable, I remember being genuinely upset that my parents wouldn't consider sending me there. It was a ridiculous request for a small-town farm kid in western New York, but it tells you something about how early this pull showed up for me.

At 18, I convinced my parents to let me use part of my college fund to take a high school trip to Italy. Standing on the Amalfi Coast, I realized something that never left me: the life I knew was not the only way to live. The culture, the pace, and the way people dressed, ate, traveled, and interacted were fundamentally different. Different realities existed, and we have the power to choose our reality.

From there came backpacking across Europe instead of an expensive exchange semester, an early marriage, and a fast track into a very "successful" life in Boston. By 24, my husband and I had done everything right: Good jobs. Financial stability. A clear path forward. And yet, I could already see the future laid out in front of us: two kids, two cars, a house in the suburbs, maybe a Cape house or a ski condo if things went well. I wasn't unhappy. I was bored.

So, when my husband suggested stepping off the career ladder to pursue a PhD in Switzerland, I said yes because it made me feel alive.

That move wasn't glamorous. I became the trailing spouse. We traded US consumerism and certainty for visas, bureaucracy, and a very unclear path forward. At the same time, FATCA/US tax compliance work was exploding, and Zurich was in desperate need of US tax professionals. Through a mix of preparation and timing, I landed in international tax, right as globally mobile Americans were starting to realize how complicated their lives had become.

That's also when money stopped feeling like numbers. Even while preparing tax returns for executives, I realized how little I understood about building a financial life abroad for myself. A well-meaning local Swiss advisor offered us products I knew, given my US compliance work, would be disastrous from a US tax perspective. Suddenly, I wasn't the professional with answers. I was just another US expat walking the tightrope: no 401(k), limited local pension access, too much cash, and no clear roadmap.

We were lucky in one way: we were young and hadn't built enough wealth for our mistakes to be too expensive. But watching clients with far more money stumble into enormous, expensive consequences made one thing very clear: complexity doesn't wait for wealth.

Looking back, my biggest blind spot wasn't ignorance. It was not having the right guidance early enough. We built up cash. We contributed to pensions that weren't optimal. We played it safe because we didn't know how to play it smart. And instead of regret, I feel compassion for that version of us. We were doing the best we could with the information we had.

This is why my work became education-first. This is why I built what I wished had existed: clear explanations, honest trade-offs, and access to real conversations, not endless googling or generic advice that doesn't apply once borders are involved. Expat lives are inherently unique. Where you're from, who you marry, how long you stay, and where you might go next all change the math. Two US expats in the same job can need completely different plans.

Today, when I think about my success abroad, it has nothing to do with optimization. It looks like driving or walking through our town on the way to the grocery store, looking up, and realizing, over and over again, that I can see the Swiss Alps. Snow-capped. Impossibly beautiful.

It looks like my children biking or walking to school on their own starting at age four. Moving around town independently. Going to the library, scouts, the pool, a friend's house, or the lake. No active shooter drills. No constant low-level fear. It feels like the version of the United State that I imagine existed in the 1970s.

That doesn't mean it's easy. There are days I ache to live closer to my parents. Close friends move back to the United States or on to another assignment. The school system is fundamentally different, more independence, less intervention, and when your child is the one being bullied, that difference can be brutal.

But at the end of the day, our family has decided the effort is worth the trade-offs. We're not waiting to see if this works. We're building a life here. And we don't anticipate moving back to the United States.

Financially, success means optionality. Not being trapped. Knowing we can adapt if life changes again. Personally, it means raising our children in a place that aligns with our values, even when it's hard. This book isn't about chasing a perfect plan. It's about understanding the system you're in, asking better questions, and making intentional choices instead of accidental ones.

If there's one thing I hope you take away, it's this: you don't need to have everything figured out. But you do need to slow down, zoom out, and remember that money is not the point.

It's the tool that supports the life you're building. And if you're reading this while standing at the beginning, still daydreaming, still researching, still unsure, I hope this book makes the path feel a little less lonely, a little less overwhelming, and a lot more possible.

If you're looking for more guidance as you navigate building life and wealth abroad, we've built resources to support you beyond this book. Through our weekly *Passport to Wealth*™ podcast, in-depth courses, blog content, and free tools, we continue these conversations and help you take the next step with more clarity.

You can explore everything at **www.PassportToWealth.com**, including resources created specifically to complement this book.

GLOSSARY

401(k) A US employer-sponsored retirement savings plan that allows employees to contribute pre-tax or after-tax income for retirement. The tax treatment of 401(k)s can become more complex once an individual lives abroad, depending on local tax laws and treaties.

529 Plan A US education savings plan that allows tax-free growth and withdrawals for qualified education expenses. Many foreign countries do not recognize the tax-free treatment, potentially taxing contributions or growth annually.

A

Active Management An investment approach in which a manager or investor makes decisions to buy, sell, or overweight specific securities in an attempt to outperform the market. Active management typically involves higher fees and greater complexity than passive investing and may introduce additional tax and behavioral risks for expats.

After-tax Return The return an investor earns after accounting for taxes owed on income, dividends, and capital gains. For expats, after-tax returns often differ significantly from pre-tax returns due to cross-border tax rules, currency effects, and differences in how investments are classified across countries.

All-weather Portfolio (Conceptual) A portfolio designed to perform reasonably well across a wide range of economic environments rather than excelling in any single scenario. In this book, the term refers to a broadly diversified, low-cost portfolio that prioritizes resilience and long-term sustainability over short-term performance.

Apostille An official certification attached to a document to verify its authenticity for use in another country. Apostilles are commonly required for documents such as birth certificates, marriage certificates, diplomas, and powers of attorney when moving abroad. The process is governed by the Hague Apostille Convention, and obtaining apostilles can add both time and cost to international relocations.

B

Behavioral Risk The risk that investor emotions, such as fear, overconfidence, or impatience, lead to poor decision-making. Behavioral risk often shows up as panic selling during market downturns, excessive tinkering, or abandoning a long-term plan. For expats, behavioral risk can be amplified by uncertainty, distance from familiar systems, and frequent life transitions.

Blocked Account/Escrow Account (for housing deposits) A restricted bank account used to hold a rental security deposit, where funds are legally protected and cannot be released without mutual agreement between tenant and landlord or a court order. Blocked or escrow-style accounts are common in many countries and are designed to safeguard both parties during and after a lease.

Bona Fide Residence Test One of the tests used to qualify for the Foreign Earned Income Exclusion. It generally requires that a US taxpayer be a bona fide resident of a foreign country for an uninterrupted period that includes an entire tax year, based on facts and circumstances such as intent, length of stay, and integration into local life.

Brokerage Account An investment account held at a financial institution that allows an individual to buy and sell securities such as stocks, bonds, exchange-traded funds, and mutual funds. Brokerage account access and available investment options can change once an individual lives outside the United States.

C

Capital Gains (Cross-border Context) The profit realized from selling an asset, calculated differently across tax systems. The US calculates capital gains in US dollars, while other countries often calculate gains in local currency, leading to mismatches.

Capital Loss Harvesting/Tax-loss Harvesting A tax strategy that involves selling investments at a loss to offset capital gains or taxable income. In cross-border situations, tax-loss harvesting must be coordinated carefully to ensure losses are recognized appropriately under both US and local tax systems.

Citizenship-based Taxation (CBT) A tax system in which a country taxes its citizens on their worldwide income regardless of where they live. Under citizenship-based taxation, US citizens are generally required to file US tax returns and report foreign income and assets even if they live abroad full-time and pay taxes in another country.

Concentration Risk The risk of having too much exposure to a single company, sector, country, currency, or employer. Concentration risk is common for expats with equity compensation, home-country bias, or assets tied to where they previously lived or worked.

Cross-border Financial Planning A holistic approach to financial planning that accounts for multiple countries, tax systems, currencies, and legal frameworks. Cross-border financial planning addresses how income, investments, taxes, retirement, estate planning, banking, and insurance interact when you live, work, or move across borders, helping individuals avoid unintended consequences and make informed decisions in a globally mobile life.

Cross-border Portfolio An investment portfolio designed to function across multiple countries and tax systems. A cross-border portfolio considers currency exposure, tax treatment in more than one jurisdiction, regulatory access, and long-term geographic mobility.

Custodian A financial institution, such as a bank or brokerage firm, that holds and safeguards investment assets on behalf of an individual. For US expats, custodians determine whether accounts can remain open abroad and which investments can be bought, sold, or held based on regulatory and compliance rules.

Custodian Risk/Platform Risk The risk that a financial institution restricts, freezes, or closes accounts due to residency, compliance, or regulatory changes. Custodian risk can lead to forced liquidations or loss of investment access for expats.

Currency of Denomination vs. Currency Exposure The currency in which an investment is traded or reported is not the same as the currencies that ultimately drive its value. Global investments may be denominated in US dollars while still carrying significant foreign currency exposure.

Currency Diversification The practice of holding assets denominated in multiple currencies to reduce exposure to fluctuations in any single currency. Currency diversification is a long-term risk management strategy, not a short-term bet on exchange rates.

Currency Risk The risk that changes in exchange rates will negatively affect the value of income, expenses, savings, or investments held in different currencies. For expats, currency risk can increase living costs or reduce purchasing power even when spending habits and income remain unchanged.

D

Direct Indexing An investment strategy that involves directly owning individual securities that make up an index rather than investing through a pooled fund. Direct indexing can sometimes provide a compliant alternative for expats who cannot access certain funds.

Discretionary Investment Management An arrangement in which an investor grants an advisor or firm authority to make investment decisions on their behalf within agreed-upon guidelines.

Double Taxation The situation in which the same income is taxed by two different countries. While this is a common fear among Americans living abroad, US tax law includes mechanisms such as exclusions, credits, and tax treaties that are designed to reduce or eliminate double taxation in many cases, though compliance and reporting requirements may still apply.

E

Elective Professional Client (EU Context) A classification under EU regulations allowing certain investors to opt out of retail investor protections. This status may permit access to restricted investment products but requires meeting specific asset or experience thresholds and involves reduced regulatory protections.

Education Savings Account (ESA) A US education-focused savings account offering tax-advantaged growth for education expenses. Like 529 plans, ESAs are often not recognized as tax-advantaged outside the United States.

Estimated Tax Payments Payments made to the IRS throughout the year on income that is not subject to withholding, such as self-employment income or investment income. US taxpayers, including expats, may be required to make quarterly estimated payments to avoid penalties and interest.

Exchange-rate Volatility The degree to which a currency's value fluctuates relative to another currency over time. High exchange-rate volatility can create unpredictable changes in monthly budgets, long-term savings, and tax outcomes for individuals living and earning across borders.

Exit Tax A tax imposed when an individual gives up US citizenship or long-term permanent resident status. The exit tax is designed to tax certain unrealized gains as if assets were sold at the time of expatriation and may apply depending on income, asset levels, and compliance history.

Expat/Expatriate A person who lives outside their country of citizenship, either temporarily or permanently. The term "expat" is commonly used to describe the lived experience of residing abroad and does not, on its own, describe a person's legal status, visa type, tax residency, or long-term intent.

Exchange-traded Fund (ETF) A pooled investment vehicle that holds a basket of securities and trades on an exchange like a stock. ETFs are commonly used for low-cost diversification but may face access or tax restrictions for US expats.

Expense Ratio The annual cost of operating an investment fund, expressed as a percentage of assets.

F

FATCA (Foreign Account Tax Compliance Act) A US law enacted in 2010 that requires foreign financial institutions to report information about accounts held by US citizens and US tax residents to the IRS. FATCA is a primary reason many foreign banks limit or refuse services to US clients due to the compliance burden.

FBAR (Foreign Bank Account Report) A separate information report filed with the US Treasury (not the IRS) that discloses foreign financial accounts. US persons must file an FBAR if the combined value of all foreign accounts exceeds $10,000 at any point during the calendar year, even if no tax is owed.

Forced Liquidation The involuntary sale of assets by a financial institution, often triggered by compliance or residency issues. Forced liquidations can create unexpected taxable events and financial disruption for expats.

Foreign Earned Income Exclusion (FEIE) A US tax provision that allows qualifying US tax residents living abroad to exclude a portion of their foreign earned income from US taxation if they meet specific residency or physical presence requirements. The exclusion applies only to earned income, not investment income, and requires an annual election on a US tax return.

Foreign Housing Exclusion/Deduction A US tax provision that allows qualifying expats to exclude or deduct certain housing expenses incurred abroad, such as rent and utilities, when claiming the Foreign Earned Income Exclusion. The amount allowed varies by location and is subject to IRS limits.

Foreign Tax Credit (FTC) A US tax provision that allows US tax residents to claim a credit for income taxes paid to a foreign country, reducing US tax owed on the same income. The foreign tax credit is commonly used by Americans abroad and can help mitigate double taxation when foreign taxes are equal to or higher than US taxes.

G

Global/International Diversification An investment strategy that spreads assets across multiple countries and regions to reduce reliance on the economic performance of any single country. For expats, international diversification can help align investments with a globally mobile lifestyle.

Green Card Holder (for tax purposes) An individual who holds lawful permanent resident status in the United States. For US tax purposes, green card holders are generally treated the same as US citizens, meaning they are subject to US citizenship-based taxation on their worldwide income and are required to file US tax returns and reporting forms, even if they live abroad.

H

Health Savings Account (HSA) A US account that allows tax-deductible contributions, tax-free growth, and tax-free withdrawals for qualified medical expenses. Outside the United States, HSAs are often treated as taxable brokerage accounts.

Home Bias The tendency to overweight investments from one's home country.

I

Internal Revenue Service (IRS) The US government agency responsible for administering and enforcing federal tax laws. The IRS oversees tax collection, tax return processing, and compliance for individuals and businesses, including US citizens and US tax residents living abroad.

IRS Form 1099 A US tax form issued by financial institutions to report income such as interest, dividends, or capital gains. While helpful for US tax reporting, Form 1099s do not always satisfy foreign tax reporting requirements.

IRS Form 1099-R A US tax form used to report distributions from retirement accounts such as IRAs and 401(k)s. These forms are designed for US tax purposes and may not align with how other countries classify or tax retirement income

IRS Form 1116 The IRS form used to claim the Foreign Tax Credit for income taxes paid to a foreign country. The form calculates the allowable credit and applies it against US tax owed on the same income.

IRS Form 2555 The IRS form used to claim the Foreign Earned Income Exclusion and, if applicable, the Foreign Housing Exclusion or Deduction. Filing this form is required each year the exclusion is claimed.

IRS Form 3520 An IRS information return used to report certain foreign gifts, inheritances, trusts, and transactions with foreign trusts. Filing requirements are based on thresholds and circumstances, and penalties for non-filing can be severe.

IRS Form 5471 An IRS information return used to report ownership or control of certain foreign corporations by US persons. This form is complex and carries significant penalties if not filed correctly.

IRS Form 8621 An IRS reporting form required for US taxpayers who own shares in a Passive Foreign Investment Company (PFIC). Each PFIC generally requires its own Form 8621, and failure to file can result in severe tax and compliance consequences.

IRS Form 8865 An IRS information return used to report ownership interests in foreign partnerships by US persons. Like Form 5471, it is highly technical and subject to substantial penalties for noncompliance.

IRS Form 8938 An IRS reporting form required under FATCA that discloses certain foreign financial assets if their value exceeds specified thresholds. Form 8938 is filed with the US tax return and is separate from the FBAR, with different thresholds and rules.

Immigrant A person who moves to a country where they are not a citizen with the intention of living there, either temporarily or permanently. The term "immigrant" is typically used in legal, administrative, and policy contexts to describe someone relocating to another country under a defined immigration framework.

Immigration Pathway The specific legal route that allows an individual to live in another country, including the visa type, residency permit, and any associated restrictions or requirements. An immigration pathway determines where you can live, whether you can work, how long you can stay, and how your tax and financial planning must be structured.

Index Fund A fund designed to track a market index rather than outperform it.

Investment Access Risk The risk that residency or regulations limit an investor's ability to buy or hold certain investments.

K

Key Information Document (KID) A standardized disclosure document required under EU regulations that provides essential information about an investment product. Many US-domiciled funds do not issue KIDs, which is why EU residents are often restricted from purchasing them.

L

Liquidity/Liquidity Risk Liquidity refers to how easily assets can be accessed or converted into cash without significant loss of value. Liquidity risk is the possibility of not being able to access cash quickly when needed, which is especially relevant for expats facing large upfront expenses, administrative delays, or currency conversion constraints.

M

Married Filing Separately (MFS) A US tax filing status used by married individuals who choose or are required to file separate tax returns. For expats, this status is sometimes used for practical or cross-border tax reasons but comes with lower filing thresholds and limited access to certain credits.

MiFID II A European Union financial regulation that governs investment services and product disclosures. Under MiFID II, many US investment products cannot be marketed or sold to EU residents because they do not provide required documentation, limiting access for US expats living in the EU.

P

Passive Foreign Investment Company (PFIC) A classification under US tax law that applies to many non-US mutual funds, exchange-traded funds, and pooled investment vehicles. PFICs are subject to punitive US tax treatment and complex reporting requirements, making them one of the most significant investment traps for US expats.

Passive Investing An investment approach focused on tracking market returns using low-cost, diversified funds.

Physical Presence Test One of the tests used to qualify for the Foreign Earned Income Exclusion. It requires that a US taxpayer be physically present in one or more foreign countries for at least 330 full days during a rolling 12-month period.

Q

Qualified vs. Ordinary Dividends A US tax distinction where qualified dividends receive preferential tax rates and ordinary dividends do not. Many countries do not make this distinction, which can cause reporting discrepancies.

R

Rebalancing (Investment Portfolio) Adjusting a portfolio back to its target allocation over time.

Residence-based Taxation (RBT) A tax system in which a country taxes individuals based on where they live and are considered tax residents rather than their citizenship. Under residence-based taxation, people generally pay income tax only in the country where they reside, and tax obligations typically end when they move abroad and establish residency elsewhere.

Residency Permit A legal status granted by a country that allows a noncitizen to reside there beyond a short-term stay. A residency permit is distinct from a visa and from tax residency, and it often governs access to healthcare, employment, housing, and social systems.

Rollover IRA An IRA created by rolling assets from a former employer's retirement plan, such as a 401(k), into an individual account. While treated similarly to a Traditional IRA in the United States, rollover accounts can have different tax or reporting implications abroad.

Roth IRA A US retirement account funded with after-tax contributions, allowing tax-free growth and withdrawals under US law. Many countries do not recognize the Roth IRA's tax-free status, which can result in unexpected taxation abroad.

S

Self-employment Tax A US tax that covers Social Security and Medicare contributions for individuals who work for themselves. US expats may still owe self-employment tax even when using the Foreign Earned Income Exclusion and/or Foreign Tax Credit, unless a totalization agreement applies.

State Tax Residency A determination of whether an individual is considered a resident of a US state for tax purposes, which can affect state income tax filing and liability. Some states maintain aggressive residency rules, making it more complex to sever state tax ties even after moving abroad.

T

Tax-advantaged Account An account that receives preferential tax treatment under a country's tax system, such as tax-deferred growth or tax-free withdrawals. An account that is tax-advantaged in one country may not receive the same treatment in another, which is a common issue for expats.

Tax Equalization A policy commonly used by employers sending employees abroad, designed to ensure that the employee pays roughly the same amount of tax as they would have paid if they had remained in their home country. Tax equalization typically benefits the employer and does not replace personal tax planning.

Tax Residency The country (or countries) in which an individual is considered a tax resident under local law, and therefore subject to taxation on some or all of their income. Tax residency is typically determined by factors such as where you live, how much time you spend in a country, where your primary home is, and where your economic and personal ties are strongest. Tax residency is different from citizenship and can change when you move.

Tax Reporting vs. Tax Liability The distinction between the obligation to report income, accounts, and assets to tax authorities and the amount of tax actually owed. For US expats, reporting requirements often continue even when little or no US tax is due, which is why compliance can feel complex despite low tax liability.

Traditional IRA A US retirement account that allows tax-deferred contributions and growth, with taxes due upon withdrawal. Some countries do not recognize the tax deferral, potentially taxing growth before distributions occur.

U

UGMA/UTMA Account Custodial accounts established for minors under US law that hold assets until the child reaches legal adulthood. These accounts can present tax, reporting, and access complications once the account holder or custodian lives abroad.

US Tax Resident An individual who is treated as a resident of the United States for tax purposes. This includes US citizens, US green card holders, and certain noncitizens who meet specific IRS tests (such as the substantial presence test). Being a US tax resident does not require living in the United States and can result in ongoing US tax filing and reporting obligations.

V

Visa An official authorization issued by a country that allows a noncitizen to enter, stay, or work for a defined period and purpose. Visas often come with conditions that affect employment rights, healthcare access, tax residency, and eligibility for long-term residency or citizenship.

W

W-2 A US tax form provided by an employer that reports wages earned and taxes withheld during the year. Many expats stop receiving W-2s once they move abroad and instead receive foreign income documentation.

INDEX

O

P

R

S